Contents

KU-712-038

English
Basics

Practice & Revision

1

CAMBRIDGE
UNIVERSITY

PUBLISHED BY THE PRESS SYNDICATE OF THE UNIVERSITY OF CAMBRIDGE
The Pitt Building, Trumpington Street, Cambridge CB2 1RP, United Kingdom

CAMBRIDGE UNIVERSITY PRESS
The Edinburgh Building, Cambridge CB2 2RU, United Kingdom
40 West 20th Street, New York, NY 10011-4211, USA
10 Stamford Road, Oakleigh, Melbourne 3166, Australia

First published 1999

Printed in the United Kingdom at the University Press, Cambridge

Typeset in Swift

A catalogue record for this book is available from the British Library

ISBN 0 521 64866 1 paperback

Layout and composition by Newton Harris Design Partnership

Illustrations by Tim Sell

Introduction

This book forms part of a three-stage series that aims to cover the 'mechanics' of the English language (spelling, punctuation and grammar) at three graded levels.

Each of the three books offers a systematic work and study programme for use in the classroom or at home.

As an introduction to the basic principles of English spelling, punctuation and grammar, Book 1 has been written specifically for children in the 9–11 age group. As a revision manual, Book 1 is also suitable for older children who need to go back over 'basics' before tackling Book 2 of this series.

The book is equally suitable for students whose first language is not English. In broad terms, Book 1 is suitable for those students who are well beyond the elementary stage of learning English but are experiencing difficulties at intermediate level.

Book 1 consists of thirty units, and each unit is divided into three sections. **Section A** consists of preliminary tasks which introduce the main topic and seek to establish the student's individual strengths and weaknesses. Having checked his/her answers to the preliminary tasks by referring to the key at the back of the book, the student is then directed to the **Reference** section. Having consulted the reference section, the student proceeds to **Section B** where the main topic is extended, revised and consolidated. A marking system is included in Section B for those students who wish to measure their progress.

The book concentrates on those areas of the English language where immediate and tangible progress can be made. As the tasks unfold, it is hoped that the student's general confidence and motivation will grow. To stimulate interest and to make the work as enjoyable as possible, many of the tasks include jokes and items of general appeal.

Although the book is designed in such a way that one can dip in at random, it is recommended that students follow the order in which the units appear. This is especially important if the book is being used for individual study.

Guidance note for teachers/parents

The tasks in Section A of each unit are 'diagnostic' in nature. Students should not worry if they make a lot of mistakes in this section as they will have plenty of opportunity in Section B to show that they have learnt from their mistakes.

Checklist of words that you need to understand

Before starting this book, make sure that you are familiar with the following words:

1   vowels and consonants
There are 26 letters in the English alphabet. These letters can be divided into vowels and consonants. The vowels are: A, E, I, O, U. All the other letters are known as consonants.

2   sentence
A sentence is a group of words that makes complete sense. It begins with a capital letter and ends with a punctuation mark. Here are two sentences:

My best friend is called Beverley. She is the same age as me.

3   verb
A verb is a 'doing' word or a 'being' word. Look at the words that have been underlined. They are verbs.

Kirsty plays three instruments. She is a very talented girl.
The cat saw the mouse and chased it across the room.

4   noun
A noun is a 'naming' word. The job of a noun is to name someone or something. Look at the words that have been underlined. They are nouns.

The boy broke the window. | Henry is my best friend. | The lion attacked the elephant.

5   pronoun
A pronoun is a word which takes the place of a noun.

Here is a sentence with two nouns: Alana does not like Leonard.
Here is the same sentence with pronouns: She does not like him.

6   adjective
An adjective tells us something more about a noun or a pronoun. Look at the words that have been underlined. They are adjectives.

an apple - a red apple; a girl - a tall girl; a book - a boring book

7   adverb

An adverb gives us more information about a verb or an adjective. Look at the words that have been underlined. They are adverbs.

She smiled. / She smiled <u>sweetly</u>.
They arrived. / They arrived <u>early</u>.
The film was good. / The film was <u>really</u> good.

8   preposition

Prepositions are words like *at, to, for, of, off, on, in, from,* etc. Prepositions only make sense when they are placed with another word. Here are some examples of how we use prepositions:

She spoke <u>to</u> me. / We stayed <u>at</u> home. / This is <u>for</u> you. / There was a box <u>of</u> chocolates <u>on</u> the table.

Starting and finishing a sentence

A

| Task 1 | Divide the words below into two sentences. Each sentence should start with a capital letter and end with a full stop. |

the fastest land mammal in the world is the cheetah it can reach speeds of over sixty miles per hour

| Task 2 | Divide the words below into three sentences. |

lions are sociable creatures they live in families rather than in big herds as other animals do in each family group there are between six and twenty animals

| Task 3 | Divide the words below into four sentences. |

snakes are cold-blooded creatures they are only as hot or cold as the air around them that is why you don't find many snakes in cool countries such as Britain it's simply too chilly for them to stay alive

Now check your answers and then consult the **Reference** section before going on to **B**.

Reference

a A sentence is a group of words that makes complete sense. There is only one way of starting a sentence. The first word of a sentence must begin with a capital letter.

b A full stop is used to mark the end of a sentence – except when you are asking a direct question (?) or making an exclamation (!).

e.g. Does anyone know where Shefali is? She is absent again. What a nuisance!

Of all the punctuation marks, the full stop is the most important. Just as a red traffic-light stops one line of traffic from crashing into another, so too the full stop prevents one sentence from running into the next. It stops one set of words from becoming confused with another.

c The exclamation mark (!) is a very 'loud' punctuation mark. We use it to express very strong emotions (like anger, shock, pleasure or amazement).

e.g. What a stupid thing to say!

B

Task 1

Correct the sentences below. Each sentence should begin with a capital letter and finish with either a question mark (?) or an exclamation mark (!).

1 what is her name
2 what a surprise
3 how embarrassing
4 how did it happen
5 do you know the answer
6 do it now

Score: /6

Task 2

Correct the advertisement below. Each sentence should start with a capital letter. Each sentence should end with a full stop.

come and enjoy a relaxing holiday at the Dolphin Hotel it is very near a clean beach and there are plenty of shops nearby the hotel is situated in a quiet area and has its own large swimming pool

the rooms are spacious and clean, and each one has its own private bath and shower with hot and cold water there is a colour TV in each room and a telephone if you want to call room service

our staff are friendly and we offer a high level of service you will find everybody helpful and cheerful there is always someone at the reception desk to help you with any problems

the hotel has two lifts there is a lounge with comfortable armchairs and a wide selection of newspapers and magazines the hotel bar never closes before two in the morning

Score: /22

2   **Showing what someone has said**

A

| Task |

In the sentences below, some of the punctuation marks are missing. Can you supply them? You will need to use speech marks ("…"), the full stop, the comma, and the question mark where appropriate. At the same time, the first word of each sentence must start with a capital letter.

1   have you seen Suzy recently

    no, I haven't seen her for ages

2   i am sure I know you he said

    i think you are mistaken she replied

    aren't you Tariq's sister he asked

    yes, I am she said

3   that jacket looks nice she said can I try it on

4   please do not touch that vase he said it's extremely valuable

Now check your answers and then consult the **Reference** section before going on to **B**.

Reference

a   Speech marks can be single or double. This book uses double for direct speech (the actual words spoken by someone). Any other punctuation mark should go inside the speech marks.

| e.g. | "How are you?" he asked. / "Get out!" he shouted.

b   We show that two different people are speaking by putting what they say on separate lines. If the spoken words are on their own, punctuation is straightforward.

| e.g. | "I enjoyed that film."
"So did I."
"What shall we do now?"
"I don't know."

c When the words in speech marks are accompanied by words like *he said*, we have to be extra careful with our punctuation.

- If the words in speech marks come first, we punctuate in the following way:

e.g.
"I am hungry," she said.
"I am hungry," she said. "Is there anything to eat?"
"I am hungry," she said, "and I am tired as well."
"I'm hungry!" she shouted.
"Are you hungry?" he asked.

- If words like *he said* come before the words in speech marks, we punctuate as follows:

e.g.
The soldier shouted, "Run for your lives!"
Then she said, "Why don't we try something else?"

B

Task 1

Correct the passage below. Use capital letters, speech marks and other punctuation marks where appropriate.

he looked at her and said where did you get that from

i found it she said it was on the floor

i don't believe you he shouted at the top of his voice

there's no need to shout she said in a firm voice

give it to me he growled or you'll be sorry   Score: /10

Task 2

Correct the joke below.

two small boys were discussing their future

what are you going to be when you grow up one of them

asked

a soldier answered the other

what if you get killed

who would want to kill me

the enemy

the other boy thought this over

okay he said when I grow up, I'll be the enemy   Score: /16

A

| Task |

Read and correct the following advert for a pen-friend. Some of the words need to start with a capital letter.

> My name is thomas smythe and I come from sheffield. I will be eleven next april. I don't have any brothers or sisters, but I've got a dog called bono.
>
> I speak a little bit of french and I know a few words in spanish (I've been to spain twice).
>
> My favourite subject at school is english and my favourite pop group is 'slick girls'.
>
> I love playing football and I support sheffield united. My ambition is to play for england!

Now check your answers and then consult the **Reference** section before going on to **B**.

Reference

a We use capital letters at the beginning of the following kinds of words:

- the names of days, months and special times of the year

e.g. Monday / July / Diwali / Christmas

   (but capitals are not necessary for the names of seasons: in summer, in autumn, in winter, in spring)

- the names of people, places and countries

e.g. Peter / Paris / Oxford Street / China

- the names of rivers, oceans and mountains

e.g. the (River) Nile / the Pacific Ocean / Mount Everest

- titles (when they are used with a name)

e.g. Mrs Doubtfire / Doctor Jekyll and Mr Hyde / Queen Elizabeth / Captain Hook

   (but: He is a doctor. / He is a captain. / Is she a princess?)

- the main words of the title of a book or film

e.g. James and the Giant Peach, Treasure Island, Independence Day, Jurassic Park

- languages, nationality and school subjects

e.g. French / Irish / Mathematics

b We also use a capital letter
- at the beginning of a sentence

e.g.   The tallest living animal is the giraffe. It lives in Africa.

- when we refer to ourselves (= I)

e.g.   I told them that I wasn't interested.

- at the beginning of direct speech

e.g.   He said, "Come along, please."

B

Task 1

Check your spelling by supplying the missing words below. Each missing word must start with a capital letter.

a   Monday, ... , ... , ... , Friday, ...
    and Sunday

b   January, ... , March, ... , May, June, ... ,
    .... , September, ... , November and ....   Score: /10

Task 2

Supply the missing words. Be careful how you spell each word and don't forget to put a full stop at the end.
    e.g. He comes from Ireland. He is Irish.

1   Ayako comes from Japan. She is ....
2   Pedro comes from Spain. He is ....
3   Angus comes from Scotland. He is ....
4   Patrick comes from Australia. He is ....
5   Bola comes from Nigeria. She is ....   Score: /5

Task 3

Underline and change any word that needs a capital letter in the two passages below. The two passages also need full stops in several places. Can you supply them?

1   my brother, tony, is a doctor he lives in wales and he speaks

    welsh fluently we usually see him at christmas and,

    sometimes, at easter

2   for many years it was thought that the nile was the longest

    river in the world in 1969, however, it was finally decided that

    the mighty amazon in south america was 4,195 miles long,

    fifty more than the nile   Score: /20

Using the comma

A

Here are three jokes. Read them aloud. The problem with these jokes is that some commas are missing. Can you work out where they should go?

1   Gary: Have you been invited to Rashid's party?
    Mike: Yes but I can't go.
    Gary: Why not?
    Mike: The invitation says 4 to 7 and I am eight.

2   "Waiter there's a dead fly in my soup."
    "Oh dear it's the hot water that kills them."

3   "Dad will you do my homework for me?"
    "No it wouldn't be right."
    "Well at least you can try."

Here are two extracts from a child's diary (describing a family holiday in Italy). There are some commas missing. Can you put them in?

1   For breakfast I had orange juice bread jam six sugar lumps hot chocolate and two crispy things.

2   The train stopped in Milan so we had to drive to Toscalano. We got there at siesta time and everything was shut so we had to wait a while.

Now check your answers and then consult the **Reference** section before going on to **B**.

Reference

a   General use of the comma:
   ● When we speak, we pause naturally at certain places. In the same way, a comma indicates a very brief pause within a sentence.

e.g.   By the way, have you seen Michael?
       Excuse me, is this the right way to the station?

   ● Quite often it is entirely up to you whether to use a comma or not. Look at the two sentences below. They are both correct. Read them aloud. Can you hear the difference between the way *of course* is being used?

Of course I'll help you.
Of course, you don't have to go if you don't want to.

b Some specific uses of the comma:
- We use commas to separate words that are listed together. In a list of words, the final two items are connected by *and* instead of a comma.

e.g.   I went on a picnic with Christopher, Mark, Nick and Sarah.

- When we use *so* to join two parts of a sentence, we usually put a comma in front.

e.g.   We arrived early, so we had to wait.
        We were late, so we missed the train.

In the examples above, *so* means 'and for that reason'.

B

Task 1   There are three commas missing in the following joke. Can you put them in?

Kelly: What's bright purple has twenty-four legs and ears that stick two inches out of its head?
Beth: I don't know.
Kelly: I don't know either but there's one crawling up your arm.   Score: /3

Task 2   Look at the following sentences. There are some commas missing. Can you put them in?

1 The moon has no atmosphere and no water so no life is possible.
2 People have been mining gold silver tin iron copper and lead for thousands of years.
3 Scientists have discovered that bees mosquitoes wasps and other stinging insects prefer to sting girls rather than boys.
4 It started to rain so we stopped playing tennis.
5 He was wearing a pink shirt green trousers and white shoes!   Score: /5

Being careful with the comma

A

What is wrong with the sentences below? Can you correct them?

1 I was sweating, I felt really uncomfortable.
2 I hate Keith, he is such a nasty boy.

Look at the six sentences below. In three of the sentences we can put a comma in the middle of the sentence to show more clearly that there are two parts to it. Which three sentences? Where exactly should the comma be placed?

1 When she heard the news she burst into tears.
2 She was very upset when she heard the news.
3 If it stops raining we'll go for a walk this afternoon.
4 We'll go down to the beach tomorrow if the weather is nice.
5 As he came nearer I became frightened.
6 We got to the station just as the train was leaving.

Now check your answers and then consult the **Reference** section before going on to **B**.

Reference

a Never use a comma to <u>join</u> two complete sentences.

    ☒ I liked the book, it was really exciting.
    ☑ I liked the book. It was really exciting.
    ☑ I liked the book because it was really exciting.

b When a sentence can be divided naturally into two parts, you can use a comma to mark that division. You do not have to use a comma, but the sentence will look clearer and neater if you do.

    A natural division will always occur in a sentence if you begin the first part of the sentence with such words as *When, As soon as, If, As, Just as, While, Before, After*.

e.g. <u>If</u> I see her at the party tonight, I'll give her the message.
<u>When</u> I got home, I had supper and went straight to bed.
<u>As</u> it grew darker, we became more frightened.

c However, you must not use a comma if you use those same words as 'joining' words in the middle of a sentence.

e.g. My father will buy me a bike <u>if</u> I pass the exam.
I got the shock of my life <u>when</u> I saw her.
I had a shower <u>as soon as</u> I got home.

B

Task 1 Correct the sentences below.

1 I didn't like the film, it was boring.
2 I don't like Karen, she's so bossy.
3 You should eat fruit, it's good for you.

Score: /3

Task 2 Supply a comma where appropriate in the sentences below. Tick any sentence where a comma is definitely not needed.

1 When I get to Paris I'll give you a ring.
2 I'll tell you when I'm ready.
3 If you don't do your homework your teacher will be annoyed.
4 We will miss the train if you don't hurry up.

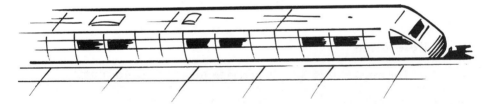

5 She telephoned me as soon as she got the news.
6 As soon as I have enough money I am going to buy a bike.
7 As it was getting late we decided to turn back.
8 Nicholas is upset because his team didn't win.
9 Our house was burgled while we were away on holiday.
10 While we were waiting for a bus we saw two foxes.
11 Just as I was leaving the postman arrived.
12 They arrived just as we were leaving.

Score: /12

6   What is the plural of 'knife'?

A

Task 1

We use the word *singular* when referring to just <u>one</u> person or thing. We use the word *plural* when referring to <u>more than one</u> person or thing. Make the following nouns plural:

1 bed - brother - sister - pen - place - shoe

2 coach - brush - bus - dress - box

3 lady - baby - body - copy - hobby

4 key - donkey - boy - toy - holiday

5 loaf - half - calf - knife - thief

Task 2

What is wrong with the following sentence?

I had fish and chips' for lunch, and then I went out to play with my friend's.

Now check your answers and then consult the **Reference** section before going on to **B**.

Reference

a For most words, simply add *-s* to make the word plural:

e.g. door/doors; window/windows; cousin/cousins

b Add *-es* to words ending in *-ch*, *-sh*, *-s*, *-ss*, *-x*. We do this so that we can pronounce the plural word clearly and easily.

e.g. church/churches; dish/dishes; minibus/minibuses; glass/glasses; fox/foxes

c For words ending in a consonant + *-y*, drop the *-y* and add *-ies*:

e.g. lorry/lorries; cherry/cherries; party/parties

d For words ending in a vowel + *-y*, keep the *-y* and just add *-s*:

e.g. journey/journeys; ray/rays; chimney/chimneys

e For words ending in *-f* or *-fe*, change the *-f* or *-fe* to *-ves*:

e.g. thief/thieves; shelf/shelves; life/lives

 Main exceptions: chiefs, handkerchiefs, roofs, cliffs

- A few words may end in either *-fs* or *-ves*:

dwarfs/dwarves; scarfs/scarves; hoofs/hooves

f Do not use an apostrophe +*-s* (*'s*) to make a noun plural:

☒ She bought some apples', pear's and orange's.
☑ She bought some apples, pears and oranges.

B

Task Change each underlined noun from singular to plural.

1 The bear was attacked by a pack of <u>wolf</u>.
2 No adult has ever actually proved that <u>elf</u>, <u>goblin</u> and <u>fairy</u> do not exist.
3 For over 1,500 years there have been <u>story</u> about a mysterious creature living at the bottom of Loch Ness in Scotland.
4 Many years ago people believed that black cats were <u>witch</u> in disguise.
5 Nearly all the large <u>city</u> in the world were once small <u>village</u>.
6 <u>Octopus</u> are not as dangerous as they look or are made out to be, but they can be unpleasant.
7 King Henry VIII had six <u>wife</u>.
8 Did you know that many <u>butterfly</u> migrate to warmer <u>country</u> in winter?
9 The air we breathe is made up of certain <u>gas</u>. Two of these, nitrogen and oxygen, make up 99% of the air.
10 There are millions of stars in just our galaxy, and there are millions of other <u>galaxy</u> in the universe.
11 A herb is a plant. Its <u>leaf</u> can be used for food, medicine, perfume, or for flavouring in cooking.
12 He ate four <u>sandwich</u>, two <u>bunch</u> of <u>banana</u>, ten <u>sausage</u> and a packet of <u>biscuit</u>. But he didn't have any ice-cream because he said he was on a diet.

13 Baby dogs are called <u>puppy</u>.

Score: /21

7   What is the plural of 'potato'?

A

Task 1

Make the nouns below plural. In each set of three, which noun is the odd one out?

a   photo - hero - video   c   piano - potato - studio
b   tomato - kilo - kangaroo   d   rhino - hippo - echo

Task 2

Make the following nouns plural:

mouse - goose - ox - foot - tooth - woman - child

Task 3

Are the underlined words singular or plural? What is strange about these words?

1   Apparently there are some 148 million <u>sheep</u> in Australia.
2   We have three <u>goldfish</u>.
3   We caught three large <u>salmon</u> in the river.
4   We saw some <u>deer</u> grazing on the hillside.

Now check your answers and then consult the **Reference** section before going on to **B**.

Reference

Is it *-os* or *-oes*?

a   For most words that end in *-o*, simply add *-s* for the plural form. These include:

- words of Spanish or Italian origin, especially those connected with music

e.g.   cello/cellos, piano/pianos, soprano/sopranos, concerto/concertos

- words where there is another vowel in front of the *-o*

e.g.   studio/studios, patio/patios, zoo/zoos, cuckoo/cuckoos, kangaroo/kangaroos

- words that are abbreviations

e.g.   rhino/rhinos (rhino = rhinoceros), hippo/hippos (hippo = hippopotamus), kilo/kilos (kilo = kilogram), photo/photos (photo = photograph)

b There are some exceptions.

- Certain words ending in -o take -es for the plural form. These include:

  domino/dominoes, echo/echoes, hero/heroes, potato/potatoes, tomato/tomatoes

- Certain words ending in -o can take either -es or -s. These include:

  mango/mangoes (or mangos), mosquito/mosquitoes (or mosquitos), tornado/tornadoes (or tornados), volcano/volcanoes (or volcanos)

c Some words do not change at all. They are both singular and plural:

e.g. one sheep / two sheep; a deer / a herd of deer; a fish / a shoal of fish

d Sometimes we have to spell a word slightly differently to show that it is plural:

e.g. foot feet, man men, goose geese, tooth teeth, ox oxen

B

Task 1 Give the plural form of the underlined words.

1 Zoo are places where wild animals are kept and exhibited.
2 Kangaroo are found in Australia.
3 Contrary to what people believe, elephants are not afraid of mouse.
4 Although clumsy on land, hippo are extremely agile in water.
5 Tomato were first introduced into Europe from Peru.
6 Roast beef with roast potato is my favourite dish.
7 Lord Nelson is regarded as one of Britain's greatest hero.
8 Rhino have been known to live for over forty years.
9 Hurricanes and tornado are the most violent storms of all.
10 Malaria is transmitted by mosquito.
11 All the islands of Hawaii are actually the tops of great volcano.
12 The suitcase weighed thirty kilo.
13 We took lots of photo on holiday.   Score: /13

Task 2 Match the phrases in column A with a suitable noun from column B, made plural.

A	B
a herd of	goose
a gang of	tooth
a gaggle of	ox
a flock of	workman
a set of false	sheep

Score: /5

8 Combining words with an apostrophe

A

Task 1

Look carefully at the piece of writing below. It is from a postcard. Some of the words need an apostrophe ('). Which ones? And where exactly should the apostrophe be placed?

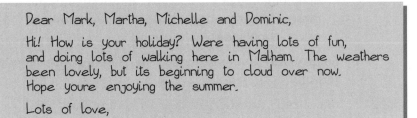

> Dear Mark, Martha, Michelle and Dominic,
>
> Hi! How is your holiday? Were having lots of fun, and doing lots of walking here in Malham. The weathers been lovely, but its beginning to cloud over now. Hope youre enjoying the summer.
>
> Lots of love,
>
> Anna, Frances, Pip and Tom.

Task 2

Read the following joke. Are all the words written correctly?

Jane: What follows a dog everywhere?
Mary: I dont know.
Jane: Its tail!

Now check your answers and then consult the **Reference** section before going on to **B**.

Reference

When we are speaking quickly, we often combine two words to form one word. When we are writing in an informal, relaxed manner, we can do the same with written English.

a To show that two words have been combined into one, we use an apostrophe ('). The apostrophe replaces one letter or more.

e.g. I'm = I am; he'll = he will; she'd = she had or she would; I don't = I do not; we didn't = we did not; he wasn't = he was not

Remember to place the apostrophe exactly where the missing letter(s) should be.

☒ She could'nt find her glasses.
☑ She couldn't find her glasses.
☒ I have'nt finished yet.
☑ I haven't finished yet.

b Note the following:

It's green. = It <u>is</u> green.
It's got three wheels. = It <u>has</u> got three wheels.
Let's go! = Let <u>us</u> go!

B

Which words need an apostrophe?

Gary: Im glad I wasnt born in France.
Mike: Why?
Gary: I cant speak French.   Score: /3

Shorten the words that have been underlined.
e.g. I think <u>she is</u> away. ➜ she's

1   She <u>does not</u> look well.
2   <u>They are</u> late again.
3   <u>That is</u> my dad over there.
4   <u>There is</u> someone at the door.
5   It looks as if <u>it is</u> going to rain.
6   <u>Who has</u> taken my jacket?
7   <u>I have</u> done my homework.
8   <u>She has</u> been absent for the past two weeks.
9   We <u>were not</u> told the truth.
10 You <u>should not</u> do that.
11 <u>Let us</u> go and see if <u>everything is</u> ready.
12 She <u>did not</u> want to go to school because she <u>had not</u> done
    her homework.   Score: /14

9 Adding -'s to a noun

A

Task 1

Look carefully at the following sentences and then answer the questions below.

1 Tania's nice.
2 Tania's mother is nice.
3 Tania's father is nice as well.
4 Tania's got a nice family.

a In which of these sentences does the apostrophe + -s ('s) show a particularly close relationship between two nouns?   b In which of these sentences does the apostrophe + -s indicate the shortened form of a verb?

Task 2

Look carefully at the following sentences. In which sentence are we talking about just one boy? How do you know? In which sentence are we talking about more than one boy? How do you know?

1 The boy's clothes were dirty.
2 The boys' clothes were dirty.

Task 3

Look at the two words that have been underlined below. What is the difference in meaning?

1 I am supposed to be at the <u>doctor's</u> in half an hour.
2 The nurses were speaking to some <u>doctors</u>.

Now check your answers and then consult the **Reference** section before going on to **B**.

Reference

a As well as showing that two words have been combined, the apostrophe is used to indicate a very close connection between two nouns (e.g. something belonging to somebody). In grammatical terms, we use the word *possession* to describe this type of relationship.

b To show this special relationship between two nouns, we normally add -'s to the first noun:

e.g. Mary's house is beautiful.
Tom's room is always untidy.

c If the first noun already has an *-s* (because it is plural), we simply add an apostrophe after the *-s*:

e.g.   This is my friend's money. (= the money belonging to a friend of mine)
This is my friends' money. (= the money belonging to some friends of mine)

d If a word is already plural but does not end in *-s* (e.g. men, women, children), we treat it like a singular noun and add *-'s*:

e.g.   the men's cloakroom / the children's toys

e Sometimes we can leave out the second noun:

e.g.   at the butcher's (= at the butcher's shop)
at the doctor's (= at the doctor's surgery)
at my gran's (= at my grandmother's house)
Susan's hair is longer than Ann's. (= Ann's hair)

B

Task

Place apostrophes where necessary in the following sentences.

1   I went straight to my uncles house.
2   Has anybody seen Kevins jacket?
3   Shelleys room was much smaller than Annas.
4   She went to the opticians to have her eyes tested.
5   My parents holiday was ruined by the weather.
6   Are you going to Fatimas party?
7   I picked up the old ladys hat and gave it back to her.
8   You should have seen the expression on Mrs Smiths face!
9   Dereks eyes were full of tears.
10   Fionas sister was wearing Surinders glasses.
11   They found the thieves hiding-place.
12   I sat down in my grandfathers armchair.

Score: /12

10 Whose, its, theirs ...

A

Task 1

Can you spot the mistake? In each of the sentences below, there is one word that should not have an apostrophe. Which one is it?

1 That bag isn't your's! It's my brother's.
2 Here's your luggage. Where's our's?
3 This isn't Yumiko's coat. Her's is brown, and this one's blue.
4 That's not our ball. It's their's.

Task 2

Select the correct alternative in brackets.

1 (Who's / Whose) at the door?
2 (Who's / Whose) bag is this?
3 (There's / Theirs) somebody outside.
4 This doesn't belong to us. It's (there's / theirs).
5 The bird flapped (it's / its) wings and flew out of (it's / its) nest.

Now check your answers and then consult the **Reference** section before going on to **B**.

Reference

a Some possessive words do not have an apostrophe:

e.g.

Whose book is it?	=	Who does the book belong to?
It's mine.	=	It belongs to me.
It's his.	=	It belongs to him.
It's hers.	=	It belongs to her.
It's yours.	=	It belongs to you.
It's ours.	=	It belongs to us.
It's theirs.	=	It belongs to them.

 Note carefully that *its* (without an apostrophe) is a possessive word:

e.g.

The hotel has its own swimming pool.
The cat licked its paw.

b Try not to confuse *whose* with *who's* (= who is / who has):

e.g.

Who's there? (= Who is there?)
Who's got my pen? (= Who has got my pen?)

26

c Try not to confuse *theirs* with *there's* (= there is / there has):

e.g.
There's some fruit on the table. (= There is ...)
There's been a mistake. (= There has been ...)

B

| Task 1 |

Change the underlined words into one word.
  e.g. It's <u>my bike</u>. → It's <u>mine</u>.

1 That's not <u>his shirt</u>. → That's not ....
2 It's <u>her ring</u>. → It's ....
3 That's <u>our car</u>. → That's ....
4 That's not <u>your pencil</u>. → That's not ....

Score: /4

| Task 2 |

Use the words that are given to complete each set of statements or questions.

a   whose / who's
   1 .... been using my pen?
   2 .... shoes are these?
   3 .... side are you on?
   4 .... that man over there?
   5 I don't care .... fault it is.

b   its / it's
   1 A leopard never changes .... spots.
   2 .... very warm in here.
   3 .... no use crying over spilt milk.
   4 The owl kills .... prey with .... claws.

c   theirs / there's
   1 .... a hole in your sock.

   2 Why are they using our machine? What's wrong with
      .... ?
   3 Is that ours or .... ?
   4 .... nothing we can do about it.

Score: /14

27

11 Adding -s to a verb

●●●

A

Task 1

A verb is a 'doing' or 'being' word. The 'doing' or 'being' may occur in the present, the past or the future. The 'tense' of a verb tells us whether we are talking about the present, past or future. Read the passage below and underline every verb you come across. Which tense is being used, the present or the past? Some of the verbs end in -s. Why?

Most lizards have long tails. When an animal catches a lizard by

its tail, the tail usually drops off and the lizard escapes. Before

long, however, a new tail grows. Lizards are cold-blooded animals.

In cold weather they bury themselves in the ground: that is how

they keep warm.

Task 2

Each of the verbs in brackets needs to end in -s. Are any other changes necessary? Write out each verb.

1 My sister (play) the piano.
2 My baby sister (cry) a lot.
3 Faisal never (pay) attention in class.
4 My mother (worry) too much.
5 My father (enjoy) fishing.
6 The Great Wall of China (stretch) for 2,150 miles.
7 My brother hardly ever (watch) television.

Now check your answers and then consult the **Reference** section before going on to **B**.

Reference

a When talking about the present, we add -s to a verb if one person or thing (he/she/it) is performing the action or being described by the verb.

b When adding -s to a verb, we apply the following rules:

● Normally we just add -s:

e.g. come (she comes); laugh (she laughs); work (it works)

● If there is a vowel in front of -y, the -y does not change when we add -s:

e.g. say (she says); play (he plays); stay (he stays)

- If there is a consonant in front of *-y*, the ending becomes *-ies* when we add *-s*:

e.g. try (he tries); study (she studies); worry (he worries)

- We add *-es* to verbs ending in *-o*, *-ss*, *-ch*, *-sh* and *-x*. We do this in order to make it easier to pronounce the word.

e.g. go (he goes); miss (she misses); watch (he watches); wash (she washes); fix (he fixes)

c The verbs 'to have' (he/she/it <u>has</u>) and 'to be' (he/she/it <u>is</u>) are irregular verbs.

B

Task

The three passages below are written in the present tense. Look at each verb in brackets. Does it need to change in any way? Tick any verb that does not need to be changed. Write out any verb that needs to be changed.

I   Breathing through lungs

Mammals (have) lungs. When we (breathe) in, air (go) through the nose and mouth and then down a long tube to the lungs. The lungs (be) like spongy bags. Inside the lungs, oxygen (pass) from the air into the blood. The blood (carry) the oxygen to every part, or cell, of the body. The other gases in the air (pass) out of the body when we (breathe) out.

Score: /8

2   The cuckoo

The cuckoo never (make) a nest. She (lay) her eggs in the nests of other birds. The cuckoo always (choose) a nest where the eggs (look) like her own. She (take) one egg from the nest and (leave) her own in its place. Then she (fly) off with the stolen egg. When the mother bird (return) to the nest, she (have) no idea that there (be) a cuckoo egg in her nest. But as soon as the eggs (hatch), the cuckoo (create) a lot of trouble because of its size and strength and (force) all the other young birds out of the nest. The mother bird then just (feed) and (care) for the young cuckoo.

Score: /15

3   The camel

When a camel (go) on a long journey, it (carry) its food with it. For days before it (start) its journey, a camel (do) nothing but eat and drink. It (eat) so much that a hump of fat (rise) on its back. The camel's body (use) up this fat during a long journey.

Score: /7

12   Adding *-ing* to a verb

A

Task

Complete each of the sentences below with the verb in brackets. Add *-ing* to each verb.

1   a   She is .... a letter. (write)
    b   We are .... to Australia. (move)
    c   Who's been .... my towel? (use)

2   a   He started .... as fast as he could. (run)
    b   I go .... every Saturday. (swim)
    c   He keeps .... on my toes! (step)

3   a   It's been .... all morning. (rain)
    b   I'm not .... very well. (feel)
    c   I hate .... potatoes. (peel)

4   a   He spent an hour .... up his room. (tidy)
    b   What are you .... ? (study)
    c   Why is he .... ? (cry)

Now check your answers and then consult the **Reference** section before going on to **B**.

Reference

a   The disappearing *-e*

- Look at the examples below. In each case, the verb ends in a consonant + *-e*. When we add *-ing*, we drop the *-e*:

smoke - smoking; prepare - preparing; make - making

- Look at the examples below. In each case, the verb ends in *-ue*. When we add *-ing*, we drop the *-e*:

pursue - pursuing; argue - arguing

 Exception: queue - queueing (or queuing)

b   Doubling the last letter (one-syllable verbs)

A one-syllable verb is a verb that is pronounced all at once (e.g. *hit*, *get*, *meet*, *put*). Look at the examples below. The final letter of each verb is a consonant. There is just <u>one</u> vowel in front of the consonant. When we add *-ing*, the final consonant doubles.

put - putting; fit - fitting; cut - cutting; win - winning;
stop - stopping

Warning! Look at the examples below. If there are <u>two</u> vowels,
the final consonant does <u>not</u> double.

beat - beating; shout - shouting; shoot - shooting;
creep - creeping

c   Verbs ending in -w, -x, -y

● Look at the examples below. The final letter of each verb is
   -w, -x, -y. When we add -ing to these verbs, the final letter
   does <u>not</u> double.

sew - sewing; box - boxing; fly - flying

B

| Task |

Complete each sentence with the verb(s) in brackets. Each verb needs to
end in -ing.

1   It's .... with rain. (pour)
2   Stop .... me! (copy)
3   It's no use .... about it. (worry)
4   My dad was .... mad when he found out what I had
    done. (hop)
5   Why are they .... that hole? (dig)
6   The audience started .... and .... (cheer) (clap)
7   We kept .... and .... on the ice. (slip) (slide)
8   She's always .... with me. (argue)
9   We're .... a party tomorrow. (have)
10 We were .... behind some bushes and saw the man
    .... the dog with a stick. (hide) (hit)
11 Are you .... to do anything special this weekend? (plan)
12 We are .... off early tomorrow morning. (set)
13 Although the sun was .... , it was .... outside.
    (shine) (freeze)
14 I was just .... ! (joke)
15 He is .... much harder this term and his work is
    certainly .... better. (try) (get)   Score: /20

13   Adding -*ed* to a verb

A

Look at the verbs that have been underlined. Are they in the present or past tense? How do you know?

In many parts of the world, people once <u>believed</u> that gods <u>lived</u> in trees. If a person <u>wanted</u> help from a tree god, he <u>reached</u> out and <u>touched</u> wood. The custom of touching wood for good luck <u>continued</u> long after people <u>stopped</u> believing in tree gods. Do you touch wood for luck?

Task 2

Put the verbs in brackets into the past tense by adding -*ed*. Be careful. You may have to make other changes as well.

1   The children (clap), (cheer) and (roar) with laughter when the clowns (start) throwing paint at each other.
2   The car (skid) on the slippery road and (crash) into a tree.
3   She (study) very hard and (try) her very best. Unfortunately, she (fail) the exam.
4   Queen Victoria, who (die) in 1901, (reign) for 63 years and 216 days.
5   At first he (stare) at me in a strange way. Then he (nod) and (smile).
6   We (stay) behind after school and (play) football in the playground.
7   He (say) that he had already (pay) the bill.

Now check your answers and then consult the **Reference** section before going on to **B**.

Reference

When adding -*ed* to a verb, try to remember the following points:

a   If a verb already ends in -*e*, just add -*d*:

e.g.   move - moved; like - liked

b   If a verb ends in a consonant + -*y*, the -*y* will change to -*i*:

e.g.   hurry - hurried; carry - carried; fry - fried

c   If a verb ends in a vowel + -*y*, the -*y* does not change:

e.g.   stay - stayed; play - played

There are three main exceptions to this rule:

say - said; pay - paid; lay - laid

d If a one-syllable verb ends in a vowel + consonant, the consonant will double:

e.g. stop - stopped; skip - skipped; hop - hopped

 If there are <u>two</u> vowels in front, the final consonant does not double:

e.g. steer - steered; clean - cleaned; rain - rained

B

Task

Add -ed to the verbs in brackets and make any other changes that may be necessary.

1 We (enjoy) our stay on the farm.
2 She (say) she really (fancy) him.
3 He (beg) me to stop.
4 Mary (cheat) in the exam! She (copy) from me.
5 She (slap) me across the face.
6 The baby (cry) all night.
7 I (step) on his toes and he (drop) the plate.
8 The dog (bury) the bone in the garden.
9 I (lay) the table while my brother (prepare) the meal.
10 They (rob) the bank and (escape) in a stolen car.
11 We (pray) for better weather.
12 You (disobey) my orders!
13 She (marry) a millionaire.
14 He (fire) the gun, but (miss) the target.
15 The box (contain) lots of toys.
16 The loud music (annoy) our neighbours.
17 He (tap) me on the shoulder.
18 Dogs have been (ban) from this park.
19 She (pour) me a drink.
20 He (rub) the words off the board.

Score: /26

14 Irregular verbs 1

A

Task 1 Put each verb in brackets into the simple past tense.
   e.g. They (dig) a big hole in our garden.
   They <u>dug</u> a big hole in our garden.

1 My mother (buy) me a new coat.
2 Yesterday my aunt (bring) us some good news.
3 The burglar (creep) up the stairs.
4 I (hear) a strange noise.
5 Suddenly I (feel) sick.

Task 2 Look at the verbs that have been underlined. In which sentences are the verbs in the present tense? In which sentences are the verbs in the past? What's strange about these particular verbs?

1 I <u>bet</u> I know the answer!
2 He <u>bet</u> £100 on a horse called 'Fortune', and it finished last!
3 Although I eat a lot of chocolate, I never <u>put</u> on weight.
4 She <u>put</u> the dress on, looked in the mirror and realised that she had <u>put</u> on weight.

Now check your answers and then consult the **Reference** section before going on to **B**.

Reference

a Usually we add -ed to a verb to put it into the past tense. There are, however, many important exceptions. Many verbs are irregular and should be learnt by heart.

b For some irregular verbs, you need to learn one extra word in order to form phrases in the past: e.g. tell - told

   I <u>told</u> her the truth. / We <u>have told</u> everybody the news. / They <u>weren't told</u> until yesterday.

   ● Here are some more examples:

   bend - bent; bring - brought; build - built; buy - bought; can - could; catch - caught; creep - crept; deal - dealt; dig - dug; feed - fed; feel - felt; fight - fought; find - found; get - got; hang - hung; have - had; hear - heard; hold - held; keep - kept; lead - led; learn - learnt; leave - left; lend - lent; lose - lost; make - made;

meet - met; sell - sold; shine - shone; shoot - shot; sit - sat; sleep - slept; slide - slid; spend - spent; stand - stood; stick - stuck; sting - stung; strike - struck; teach - taught; think - thought; win - won

c Some one-syllable verbs do not have a separate past form. The verb remains the same in the past: e.g. set - set

I normally <u>set</u> off for school at 8.30. Yesterday, I <u>set</u> off at 8.15.

● Here are some more examples of verbs that do not have a separate past form:

bet; bid; burst; cast; cost; cut; hit; hurt; let; put; read; shut; split; spread; upset

B

Task 1

The following verbs in brackets need to be in the past tense. Change the form of the verb where necessary. Tick any verb that does not need to change.

1 We (catch) the first available train, but then (find) we had (get) on the wrong train.
2 I got (sting) by a bee and it really (hurt).
3 At half-time the score was 4-nil, and we (think) we had (lose) the match. But in the second half we (fight) back really hard and (win) the game by five goals to four.
4 My little brother (spread) the butter all over his face and we all (burst) out laughing.
5 We (hold) hands as we (slide) down the muddy hill.
6 They (keep) on teasing me.
7 When he (bend) down, he (split) his trousers.
8 I was (teach) to swim by my father.
9 She (stick) her tongue out at me, and that (make) me really mad.
10 We (spend) the whole day on the beach and (build) a huge sandcastle that (can) be seen for miles around.   Score: /22

Task 2

Correct any spelling mistakes in the sentences below.

1 In 1912 the Titanic was the largest ship that had ever been bilt.
2 Everybody thougt that the ship was unsinkable.
3 On her first voyage, the Titanic struk an iceberg and sank.   Score: /3

15 Irregular verbs 2

A

| Task |

Change each verb in brackets into its correct past form. In each case, use just one word.

1 I was so tired that I (fall) asleep immediately.
2 I have often (fall) asleep in class.
3 Yesterday a dog (bite) my brother on the leg.
4 I have never been (bite) by a dog.
5 He (begin) to cry when I told him the news.
6 The film hasn't (begin) yet.
7 He (hide) the key under a stone.
8 The police discovered that the thieves had (hide) the money under the kitchen floor.
9 He was so thirsty that he (drink) three bottles of lemonade in five minutes.
10 He said that it was the first time he had (drink) cider.

Now check your answers and then consult the **Reference** section before going on to **B**.

Reference

a For some irregular verbs, you need to learn two words in order to form phrases in the past tense.

e.g. give: gave - given

b When learning the two past forms of these particular verbs, remember that the first form stands on its own (e.g. he gave) and the second form is usually accompanied by another verb (e.g. I <u>have</u> given; I <u>was</u> given).

● Here are some further examples of this type of irregular verb. Study carefully the spelling of the words listed below.

<u>beat</u> - beat - beaten; <u>begin</u> - began - begun; <u>bite</u> - bit - bitten; <u>blow</u> - blew - blown; <u>break</u> - broke - broken; <u>choose</u> - chose - chosen; <u>come</u> - came - come; <u>do</u> - did - done; <u>draw</u> - drew - drawn; <u>drink</u> - drank - drunk; <u>drive</u> - drove - driven; <u>eat</u> - ate - eaten; <u>fall</u> - fell - fallen; <u>fly</u> - flew - flown; <u>forget</u> - forgot - forgotten; <u>freeze</u> - froze - frozen; <u>go</u> - went - gone; <u>grow</u> - grew - grown; <u>hide</u> - hid - hidden; <u>know</u> - knew - known; <u>ride</u> - rode - ridden; <u>rise</u> - rose - risen; <u>run</u> - ran - run; <u>see</u> - saw - seen; <u>shake</u> -

shook - shaken; <u>sing</u> - sang - sung; <u>sink</u> - sank - sunk; <u>speak</u> -
spoke - spoken; <u>steal</u> - stole - stolen; <u>swim</u> - swam - swum; <u>take</u> -
took - taken; <u>tear</u> - tore - torn; <u>throw</u> - threw - thrown; <u>wear</u> -
wore - worn; <u>write</u> - wrote - written

B

| Task 1 | Select the correct alternative in each case. |

1   I almost cried when she (sang / sung) my favourite song.
2   She said that she had never (sang / sung) in front of an
    audience before.
3   I've (spoke / spoken) to her on several occasions.
4   We've (ran / run) out of milk.
5   I'm afraid I (forgot / forgotten) her birthday.
6   I bet she's (forgot / forgotten) all about it.
7   I'm sure I (saw / seen) her yesterday.
8   She (swam / swum) the English Channel in six hours.
9   The ship (sank / sunk) to the bottom of the sea.
10 "I (did / done) it," he admitted.
11 "I've (did / done) it," he announced.
12 He has never (rode / ridden) a bicycle.
13 Somebody's (took / taken) her pen.
14 Somebody (came / come) in and (took / taken) my bag.
15 Tom: Did you hear about the thief who (stole / stolen) a
            calendar?
    Mike: No, what happened?
    Tom: He got twelve months!   Score: /16

| Task 2 | Check your spelling by selecting the correct alternative in each case. |

1   He (toor / tore) his trousers.
2   I (new / knew) she would be angry.
3   Have you (writen / written) to her?
4   We (flu / flew) to Greece.
5   The referee (blew / blue) his whistle.
6   That's not the one I wanted. You (choose / chose) the wrong
    one!
7   He (war / wore) his best clothes for the occasion.
8   He (shook / shock) my hand.
9   She (broke / brocke) her leg in the accident.
10 England was (beaten / beeten) 2-0 by Spain.   Score: /10

16   Adjectives

Task 1

A

What is an adjective? Look at the jokes below. How many adjectives can you find? Underline them.

1   Secretary: What silly fool put these flowers on my desk?
    Boss: I did.
    Secretary: Oh, aren't they lovely?

2   Customer: This steak is terrible. I want the manager!
    Waiter: I am sorry, sir. He's not on the menu.

3   Aunt: Eat all your vegetables and you'll grow up to be a very
           pretty and intelligent girl.
    Niece: Didn't you eat any vegetables when you were little then?

Task 2

How many spelling mistakes can you find in the jokes below?

1   Man: I'd like to order a piece of steak as tuff as old leather,
            some peas as hard as bullets, and a helping of greasey
            chips.
    Waiter: Oh sir, we couldn't possibly serve you anything as
            awfull as that.
    Man: Why not? That's what you gave me yesterday.

2   Customer: This soup's a bit funney.
    Waiter: Really? So why aren't you laughing?

3   Brother: Last night I dreamt I was dancing with the most
             beautifull girl in the world.
    Sister: Really? What was I wearing?

Now check your answers and then consult the **Reference** section before going on to **B**.

Reference

a An adjective is a word that describes something or someone.
    The words *big* and *nice* are adjectives.

b Sometimes it is difficult to remember how to spell an adjective
    because of the way it is pronounced. Such words need to be
    learnt by heart.

e.g.   tough / rough / straight (pronounced 'tuff' / 'ruff' / 'strait')

c Some common adjectives cause spelling problems because there are double letters within the word. Again, such words need to be learnt by heart.

e.g. sorry, possible, difficult, different, necessary, horrible, terrible

d There are, however, some spelling rules which will make life easier for you when using adjectives.

● When the word *full* is added to another word, the last *-l* is dropped. That is why there is only one *-l* at the end of such adjectives as *careful, beautiful, awful, painful* ...

● When we add *-y* to a word ending in *-e*, the *-e* usually disappears:

e.g. grease - greasy; noise - noisy; rose - rosy; scare - scary

● When we add *-y* to a one-syllable word that ends in one vowel + consonant, the consonant doubles:

e.g. sun - sunny; fog - foggy; fun - funny

 Note that there is no *-e* in front of the *-y*. Very few adjectives end in *-ey* (e.g. grey). Most words that end in *-ey* are <u>nouns</u> rather than adjectives (e.g. monkey, turkey, donkey).

B

Task

There is at least one spelling mistake in each of the following sentences. Underline and correct each mistake.

1 I was feeling hungrey and thirsty.
2 She got angrey with me and said some really horible things.
3 Although the weather was awfull, we had a wonderfull holiday.
4 I've got short wavey hair and rosey cheeks.
5 My brother's got long straite hair.
6 I'm usually cheerfull and easygoing, but I have a nastey temper.
7 My brother's quite shy and doesn't like noisey parties.
8 The stoney path was really ruff on our feet and I was quite glad when we reached the grassy hillside.
9 It was dificult to tell whether I had a cold or flu. I had a runy nose and a terible cough. On the other hand, my temperature was normal.
10 The food was tastey.
11 That's not posible, is it?
12 The operation was painfull but necesery.

Score: /20

17 Adjectives ending in *-ing* / *-ed*

Task

A

Rewrite each word in brackets so that it ends in either *-ing* or *-ed*.

1 I found the book very (bore).
2 I'm not (interest) in sport.
3 It's an (amaze) story.
4 He wasn't (satisfy) with what I said.
5 It was quite an (amuse) film.
6 I'm sorry, but I'm not (amuse). That wasn't funny.
7 She is (annoy) with me because I didn't help her.
8 What's that (annoy) noise?
9 This report is really (please).
10 She is (please) with my progress.
11 The news is rather (worry).
12 She had a (worry) expression on her face.

Now check your answers and then consult the **Reference** section before going on to **B**.

Reference

a Adjectives may end in *-ing* or *-ed*:

e.g. This lesson is boring. / I am bored.

To form such adjectives, we apply the same rules used for forming verbs ending in *-ing* or *-ed*.

b When adding *-ing*, remember:

• we drop the *-e* if the word ends in consonant + *-e*

e.g. amuse - amusing

• *-y* does not change

e.g. worry - worrying

c When adding *-ed*, remember:

• if there is already an *-e*, just add *-d*

e.g. amuse - amused

• *-y* + *-ed* becomes *-ied* if there is a consonant in front of the *-y*

e.g. worry - worried

40

d Adjectives ending in *-ing* are often used to describe what someone or something is like:

e.g. It is interesting. / He is good-looking. / He is charming.

e Adjectives ending in *-ed* are often used to describe a person's feelings:

e.g. I am pleased. / I was shocked. / He looks frightened.

f Certain adjectives are so common that you should make absolutely sure that you do not misspell them. Learn the following by heart:

annoying/annoyed; boring/bored; depressing/depressed; disappointing/disappointed; disgusting/disgusted; embarrassing/embarrassed; exciting/excited; frightening/frightened; horrifying/horrified; shocking/shocked; surprising/surprised; terrifying/terrified; worrying/worried

B

Task

Check your spelling. Underline and correct any adjective that has been misspelt. Place a tick against any sentence that does not contain a spelling mistake.

1 I was suprised to see her again.
2 The children were getting exited because it was almost the end of term.
3 It was the most boreing film I had ever seen.
4 The storm was really terifying and we hid under our beds.
5 We were terrified of our new teacher.
6 It was such an embarassing situation that I went as red as a beetroot.
7 I was too embarrased to tell her the truth.
8 What depressing weather!
9 She looked quite shoked when she came out of the room.
10 The food was desgusting and we refused to eat it.
11 My teacher said she wasn't satisfyed with my explanation.
12 Our teacher was horrorfied when he found out what we had done.
13 It was a fritening experience and I shall never go back there again!
14 We were all very dissapointed when the trip was cancelled.
15 He has the annoying habit of chewing his nails when reading.
16 She looks worried. Do you think there is something wrong? Score: /16

18   Making adjectives negative

A

Task

Write down one word in place of the two given. In each case, you will have to supply an adjective beginning with *il-, im-, in-, ir-, un-* or *dis-* .

e.g.   not comfortable = uncomfortable

1	not possible =		6	not important =
2	not legal =		7	not necessary =
3	not regular =		8	not mature =
4	not honest =		9	not patient =
5	not usual =		10	not visible =

Now check your answers and then consult the **Reference** section before going on to **B**.

Reference

a   Many adjectives can be made negative by adding a prefix to them. A prefix is a letter or group of letters added to the beginning of a word to make a new word.

e.g.   happy - <u>un</u>happy (*un-* = a negative prefix)

b   Understanding the use of negative prefixes will help you to improve your spelling.

e.g.   *un-* + necessary = <u>un</u>necessary; *dis-* + satisfied = <u>dis</u>satisfied

c   Which negative prefix goes with which adjective?

Certain adjectives follow a particular pattern. Many common adjectives, however, need to be learnt by heart.

d   *ir-, il-, im-*

These three prefixes follow a particular pattern with some adjectives.

● The prefix *ir-* is added to certain adjectives beginning with *r*:

e.g.

(ir)regular; (ir)responsible; (ir)relevant

Some exceptions: (un)reliable; (un)reasonable

● The prefix *il-* is added to certain adjectives beginning with *l*:

e.g.

(il)logical; (il)legal; (il)legible; (il)literate

Some exceptions: (un)lucky; (un)limited

- The prefix *im-* is added to certain adjectives beginning with *m* or *p*:

e.g. (im)moral; (im)mature; (im)possible; (im)polite

Some exceptions: (un)popular; (un)pleasant

e *in-, dis-, un-*

These three prefixes do not follow a predictable pattern. The commonest prefix is *un-*. Adjectives taking *in-* and *dis-* should be learnt by heart:

e.g. *in-*: (in)accurate; (in)expensive; (in)effective; (in)efficient; (in)capable; (in)secure
dis-: (dis)loyal; (dis)honest; (dis)respectful
un-: (un)occupied; (un)necessary; (un)official

B

Task

1 Complete each adjective below with *in-* or *un-*:

an ......efficient secretary; an ......grateful child; an ......convenient moment; an ......curable disease; an ......formal interview; an ......even surface; an ......expensive present; an ......fair decision; an ......accurate answer

Score: /9

2 Complete each adjective below with *im-* or *un-*:

an ......polite remark; an ......popular decision; an ......pleasant sight; an ......patient teacher

Score: /4

3 Complete each adjective below with *ir-, il-* or *un-*:

......responsible parents; an ......reliable worker; an ......reasonable request; ......legible handwriting; an ......literate peasant; ......lucky numbers

Score: /6

4 Complete each adjective below with *dis-* or *un-*:

......obedient children; ......satisfactory work; ......respectful students; ......loyal workers; ......fortunate results

core: /5

19   Adding *-er* / *-est* to an adjective

A

Task 1 Rewrite the adjectives in brackets so that they end in *-er*. You will need to decide if any spelling changes are required when you add *-er* to each word.

1. Most scientists believe that the Earth is getting (warm).
2. The Sahara desert is (large) than Australia.
3. Peter may be (fat) than most of the other students in the class, but I reckon he is much (fit) and (strong) than most of them!

Task 2 Rewrite the adjectives in brackets so that they end in *-est*. You will need to decide if any spelling changes are required when you add *-est* to each word.

1. The Arctic is the (small) of the oceans, and the Pacific is the (large).
2. She blushed when he told her that she was the (pretty) girl in the class.
3. Graham is definitely the (lazy) boy in the class!

Now check your answers and then consult the **Reference** section before going on to **B**.

Reference

a If an adjective ends in *-er*, this tells us that a comparison is being made.

e.g.   He is taller than his mother.

b If an adjective ends in *-est*, this tells us that a particular person or thing is being singled out from a group of people or things.

e.g.   Paul is the tallest boy in the class.

c We add *-er* or *-est* to one-syllable adjectives (e.g. fat, thin) and to two-syllable adjectives ending in *-y* (e.g. easy, pretty). For most other two-syllable adjectives and for all other long-sounding adjectives, we use *more* and *most*.

e.g.   This chair is more comfortable than that one. / This is the most interesting book I have ever read.

d We apply the following rules when adding *-er* or *-est* to an adjective:

- For words of one syllable ending in -e, just add -r or -st:

e.g. large - larger - largest; safe - safer - safest

- For words of one syllable ending in one vowel + consonant, the final consonant is doubled:

e.g. fit - fitter - fittest; thin - thinner - thinnest

- For words of one syllable ending in two vowels + consonant, the final consonant is <u>not</u> doubled:

e.g. great - greater - greatest; cool - cooler - coolest

- When -er or -est is added to an adjective ending in a consonant + -y, the -y becomes -i:

e.g. easy - easier - easiest; pretty - prettier - prettiest; lazy - lazier - laziest; dry - drier - driest

B

| Task |

Decide whether each adjective in brackets should end in -er or -est. Write out each adjective.

1 The Moon is much (small) and (light) than the Earth.
2 Some of the world's (big) mountains are on the sea bed. Some undersea mountains are (tall) than those on land.
3 Some seas are (salty) than others. The Dead Sea, between Jordan and Israel, is so salty that no fish can live in it.
4 As you climb up a mountain, the air becomes (thin) and it becomes (hard) to breathe. That's why mountaineers carry extra oxygen with them.
5 More than 120 million people cross the border between Mexico and the USA every year, making it the (busy) frontier in the world.
6 Deserts are the (hot) and (dry) places on Earth. The Antarctic is the (cold) and (windy) place in the world.
7 The (wide) road in the world is the Monumental Axis in Brasilia, Brazil. It is 250 metres wide, which is wide enough for 160 cars side by side.
8 "What's the (cheap) and (easy) way to see the world?" "Buy an atlas!"
9 "What is the (dirty) word in the world?" "Pollution!"
10 "Which word grows (small) when you add letters to it?" "I don't know." "Short. When you add -er to short, it becomes (short)!"

Score: /18

20 Adverbs ending in -ly

A

Task 1

Which words below are adverbs? Underline them.

1 My younger sister sings beautifully.
2 The old man drove carefully.
3 The tall woman spoke quietly and calmly.
4 It rained heavily.

Task 2

Correct the following sentences:

1 He drove slow.
2 I was real glad to see her.
3 They beat us easy.
4 He spoke to her as gentle as possible.

Now check your answers and then consult the **Reference** section before going on to **B**.

Reference

a What is an adverb?

● An adverb adds extra information to a verb.

e.g. He smiled. / He smiled <u>nervously</u>.

● An adverb can strengthen or weaken an adjective.

e.g. He is ill. / He is <u>seriously</u> ill.
I was surprised. / I was <u>slightly</u> surprised.

● An adverb can accompany a whole phrase or sentence.

e.g. Nobody was injured. / <u>Fortunately</u>, nobody was injured.

b Forming adverbs ending in -ly

Many adverbs end in -ly. To form such adverbs, we start with an adjective as our base word and then add -ly.

e.g. slow - slowly; quick - quickly

c Points to note:

● If an adjective already ends in -l, we will end up with -lly.

e.g.   normal - normally; careful - carefully; usual - usually

- If an adjective ends in *-le*, we drop the *-e* and just add *-y*.

e.g.   incredible - incredibly; terrible - terribly; gentle - gently

- If an adjective ends in *-e* (apart from *-le*), we usually keep the *-e*.

e.g.   safe - safely; extreme - extremely; nice - nicely

(Exception: true/truly)

- If an adjective ends in *-y*, we will end up with *-ily*.

e.g.   heavy - heavily; lucky - luckily; happy - happily

(Exceptions: shy/shyly; sly/slyly)

- If an adjective ends in *-ic*, we will end up with *-ally*.

e.g.   automatic - automatically; basic - basically

(Exception: public/publicly)

B

Task

Complete each sentence by forming an adverb from the adjective in brackets.

1 The doctor saw me .... (immediate)
2 She reacted .... to the news. (angry)
3 He .... set fire to her dress. (accidental)
4 He is .... strong. (incredible)
5 ...., nobody was hurt. (lucky)
6 It's .... cheap! (fantastic)
7 The building was .... destroyed in the fire. (complete)
8 He .... doesn't want to see you. (probable)
9 She .... needed some help. (desperate)
10 She is .... upset. (terrible)
11 Could you .... come in earlier tomorrow? (possible)
12 We .... have fish for supper on Fridays. (usual)
13 .... we heard a scream. (sudden)
14 They are .... married. (happy)
15 ...., he is not well. (unfortunate)
16 She's .... on time. (normal)   Score: /16

21 Some tricky nouns

A

Task 1 Select the correct alternative in the brackets below.

1 He doesn't realise just how strong he is. In other words, he doesn't know his own (strength/strenth/strenght).
2 Her hair comes down to her shoulders. In other words, she has shoulder-(lenth/length/lenght) hair.
3 If we want to know how heavy something is, we check its (weight/wait/weigth).
4 On a passport, you have to state your (height/hight/heigth).

Task 2 Change the words below into 'person' nouns by adding one of the following endings: *-er, -or, -ar*.
   e.g. a photograph......... ➜ a photographer

1	a visit.........	6	a spectat.........
2	a garden.........	7	a lawy.........
3	a conduct.........	8	an act.........
4	a butch.........	9	a teach.........
5	a burgl.........	10	a li.........

Now check your answers and then consult the **Reference** section before going on to **B**.

Reference

a It is not always easy to remember how to spell certain nouns. One way of remembering is to group particular nouns together.

e.g. <u>Strong</u> and <u>long</u> (adjectives) become <u>strength</u> and <u>length</u> (nouns).
<u>Height</u> and <u>weight</u> (nouns) have the same spelling as number 8 (= <u>eight</u>).
<u>Deep</u> and <u>wide</u> (adjectives) drop an *e* when they become nouns: <u>depth</u> and <u>width</u>.

b Many nouns in English have one of the following endings: *-er, -or, -ar*.

When referring to a person, these endings (*-er, -or, -ar*) mean 'a person who ...':

e.g. a teacher = a person who teaches

an inventor = a person who invents

- The most common of these three endings is -er:

e.g.   builder, carpenter, driver, farmer, hunter, manager, painter, worker

- There are, however, a large number of 'person' nouns that end in -or:

e.g.   actor, author, competitor, conductor, decorator, director, doctor, editor, inspector, instructor, inventor, operator, sailor, spectator, tailor, traitor, translator, visitor

Words that end in -or should be learnt by heart. If you look back at the examples, you will see that the majority of these words end in -tor.

- There are very few 'person' nouns ending in -ar. The most common ones are:

e.g.   beggar, burglar, liar, scholar

B

Task 1

Make the words below into 'person' nouns by adding one of the following endings: -er, -or, -ar.

1 a trait.........
2 a begg.........
3 a prison.........
4 a doct.........
5 a police inspect.........
6 a football play.........
7 a telephone operat.........
8 an experienced travell.........
9 a sail.........
10 an old-age pension.........
11 a driving instruct.........
12 a bank robb.........
13 a long-distance swimm.........
14 an interior decorat.........
15 a professional ski.........

Score: /15

Task 2

Complete the sentences below with nouns formed from the words in brackets.

1 She managed to swim one .... of the swimming-pool, but didn't have the .... to continue. (long) (strong)
2 The nurse checked his .... and .... (high) (weigh)
3 If you are not a good swimmer, don't go out of your .... (deep)
4 We had to measure the .... of the floor. (wide)

Score: /6

49

Who / which / whose / whom

Task 1   Complete the sentences below with *who* or *which*.

1   Mushrooms are fungi. Fungi are plants .... do not have green leaves or flowers.
2   I didn't know many of the people .... came to the party.
3   A waiter is someone .... works in a restaurant.
4   Thirteen is a number .... many people consider to be unlucky.
5   Do you know anybody ....can help me with this problem?

Task 2   Complete the sentences below with *who* or *whose*.

1   Look! That's the man .... stole her purse.
2   Look! That's the woman .... purse was stolen.
3   There was once a farmer .... name was Bill.
4   There was once a farmer .... lived on the edge of a forest.

Task 3   Complete the sentences below with *who* or *whom*.

1   I'd like to know .... gave you that information.
2   .... did you get that information from?
3   From .... did you obtain that information?
4   .... is he talking to?
5   With .... am I speaking?

Now check your answers and then consult the **Reference** section before going on to **B**.

Reference

a   *who / which*

We can use *who* or *which* as 'joining' words (like links in a chain!). The important point to remember is that *who* comes immediately after a 'person' noun or pronoun, and *which* comes immediately after any other type of noun.

e.g.   I think it was <u>Michael who</u> phoned. ('Michael' = a 'person' noun)
A saltwater fish is <u>a fish which</u> can only live in the sea. ('a fish' is not a person)

b *who / whose*

We saw in Unit 10 that *whose* is a 'possessive' word. We can use *whose* as a 'joining' word. This happens when we want to show a *possessive* relationship between a 'person' noun and a noun that immediately follows.

e.g.   At the concert last night, I spoke to <u>a boy whose brother</u> plays in a group.

c *who / whom*

Whom is a very formal word. In the old days, there were many complicated rules for when you should or shouldn't use *whom*. Nowadays, we are more relaxed about the word. All you need to remember is that *who* becomes *whom* when you have a preposition in front of *who*. Prepositions are small words like *in*, *with*, *to*, *from*, *by*.

e.g.   <u>Who</u> is she going out with? (= normal, informal English)
<u>With whom</u> is she going out? (= very formal English)

B

Task   Complete the gaps below with *who, which, whose* or *whom*.

1   The African ostrich, ... is the largest of all living birds, cannot fly at all.
2   Some crocodiles will not only attack anyone .... comes near them in the water, but they will run up on the land in pursuit of their victims, grab them, and then carry them back into the water!
3   The jellyfish is an animal .... doesn't have a skeleton. It doesn't have a brain either!
4   Jogging is an activity .... is good for your health.
5   That's the girl .... took my bicycle.
6   That's the girl .... bicycle was stolen.
7   Ann: I've just received some money.
    Sue: .... from?
8   Dave: I've just received some money.
    Mark: From ....?
9   In the United Kingdom there is only one poisonous snake, the adder, ... is found in most parts of the British Isles (but not in Ireland).
10 People say that John Montagu, the 4th Earl of Sandwich (1718–92), was the man .... invented sandwiches.

Score: /10

Spoken and written English 1

A

| Task |

Below you will find some examples of informal speech. In each case there is a grammatical error. What are the mistakes? Can you correct them?

1 The thing what annoys me is the way she talks about me behind my back.
2 I didn't see nobody.
3 There's no point in asking her. She don't know.
4 A dishwasher is a machine what washes dishes.
5 Me and Susan, Ayesha, Sarah and Kiran went to a disco on Saturday night.
6 I don't remember nothing.
7 Me and my brother go swimming every Saturday.
8 We was robbed!

Now check your answers and then consult the **Reference** section before going on to **B**.

Reference

There are certain grammatical mistakes which are very common in informal speech. Be aware of these mistakes and try to avoid making them in your writing.

a *What* + verb

Never use *what* as a 'joining' word between a noun and a verb:

 ☒ That's the boy <u>what</u> stole my bike.
 ☑ That's the boy <u>who</u> stole my bike.
 ☒ The only thing <u>what</u> I didn't like was the food.
 ☑ The only thing (<u>that/which</u>) I didn't like was the food.

If you are ever in doubt, just remember that *what* + verb means 'the thing that':

| e.g. |

A camcorder is <u>what</u> I'd like most for my birthday.

<u>What</u> I'd like for Christmas is a new bike.

b Double negatives

Be really careful when using 'negative' words (such as *no, no one, nobody* and *nothing*). Since these words are negative, they do not require a negative verb.

e.g.   I saw nobody. / I saw no one. / He did nothing. / There is no milk left.

If we decide to make the verb negative, then *no* + word becomes *any* + word.

e.g.   I didn't see anybody. / I didn't see anyone. / He didn't do anything. / There isn't any milk left.

c *My brother and I | me and my brother*

Before a verb, use *I*. After a verb or preposition, use *me*.

e.g.   My brother and I built a snowman in the back garden.
She brought some presents for me and my brother.

d *don't/doesn't, was/were*

Make absolutely sure that you use the correct part of a verb:

e.g.   I don't; you don't; we/they don't; he/she/it <u>doesn't</u>
I was; he/she/it was; we <u>were</u>; you <u>were</u>; they <u>were</u>

B

Task 1

Complete the following statements with *that* or *what*.

1 The thing .... surprised us was her attitude.
2 .... surprised us was how calmly he took the news.
3 The only thing .... I don't like about her is that she can be a bit bossy.
4 .... I like about her is her lovely sense of humour.
5 Everything .... she has said is absolutely true.
6 Those are not the shoes .... I ordered.

Score: /6

Task 2

Select the correct alternative in brackets.

1 There was (nobody / anybody) at home.
2 There wasn't (nobody / anybody) there.
3 They found (nothing / anything) out of place.
4 They didn't find (nothing / anything) unusual.
5 There is (no / any) need to speak to me like that.
6 He hasn't got (no / any) money.
7 Andrew and (me / I) are in the same team.
8 You can play with Andrew and (me / I) if you like.
9 You (were / was) right.
10 My mum (don't / doesn't) allow me to go out by myself.

Score: /10

● ●

A

Task 1

Rewrite the sentences below in standard written English.
e.g. "Get outta here!" = "Get out of here!"

1 "I dunno who dunnit."
2 "I wanna be a pop star."
3 "Who's gonna tell her?"

4 "I've gotta go now."
5 "Are you alright?"

Task 2

Underline and correct any spelling mistakes in the sentences below.

1 "I didn't go to school last fursday because I had toofache."
2 "I fought my bruvver would be home, but he wasn't."
3 "There are firty children in my class."

Task 3

Pronounce the words below. Are they spelt correctly?

1 a villige; 2 the cinima; 3 a presant; 4 a discription;
5 to dicide; 6 a sootcase; 7 ten minites; 8 an English dictionery;
9 English grammer; 10 the town center

Now check your answers and then consult the **Reference** section before going on to **B**.

Reference

Unlike many other languages, the English language is not always written in the same way as it is pronounced or spoken.

a In informal speech, people often say things like *gonna*, *wanna*, *gotta*, *dunno*.

In standard written English, these words should be written as *going to*, *want to*, *got to* and *don't know*.

b Normally, *all* becomes *al* when added to another word:

e.g. almost, altogether, always, already

However, you should always spell *all right* as two separate words. The spelling *alright* is not acceptable in standard written English.

c In informal speech, the letters *th* are often mispronounced and may sound like *f* or *v*.

e.g. "my muvver"; "he's a fief"; "I fink"

In standard written English, spellings must be correct:

e.g. my mo<u>th</u>er; he's a <u>th</u>ief; I <u>th</u>ink

This is particularly important with words that may change their meaning if you misspell them:

e.g. fought/thought; deaf/death; fin/thin; free/three

d Vowel sounds are tricky in English. Spelling mistakes are often made when we simply write down words as they sound.

e.g.

- ✗ villige, cottige, cabbige, grammer, calender
- ✔ village, cottage, cabbage, grammar, calendar
- ✗ center, theater (= American English)
- ✔ centre, theatre
- ✗ color, favorite, neighbor (= American English)
- ✔ colour, favourite, neighbour
- ✗ responsable, definate, seperate, oppisite
- ✔ responsible, definite, separate, opposite

Be aware of this problem and, when in doubt, use a dictionary.

B

| Task |

Underline and correct any word that has been misspelt in the sentences below. There is one mistake in each sentence.

1 Will they be alright on their own?
2 They were allready there when we arrived.
3 Did she receive the messige?
4 We took too much luggige with us.
5 We are definately not going back to that village.
6 We live in a cottage oppisite a park.
7 My best friend gave me a camara for my birthday.
8 My mother's favorite programme is 'Neighbours'.
9 My grandfather doesn't have a colour telivision.
10 Our teacher taught us some grammer yesterday.
11 I often go to the cinema, but I've never been to the theater.
12 The doctor told me I was too fin and needed to eat more.
13 I share a bedroom wiv my younger sister.
14 My two brothers have seperate bedrooms.
15 Who's responsable for all this mess?

Score: /15

25   Of / off, into, out of ...

A

Task 1   Select the correct alternative in brackets.

1   He's just bought a new set (of / off) tools.
2   We set (of / off) at six o'clock the following morning.
3   A bottle is made (of / off) glass.
4   They made (of / off) with all our money.
5   He fell (of / off) his bicycle.

Task 2   Correct the sentences below.

1   He threw it out the window.
2   He took a shirt out the drawer.
3   They pushed him in the pond.
4   He jumped in to the river.

Now check your answers and then consult the **Reference** section before going on to **B**.

Reference

a   *of | off*

When distinguishing between the prepositions *of* and *off*, try to remember the following basic points:

- The two words are pronounced differently: *of* ends in a hard sound (= *v*), whereas *off* has a gentle *f* sound.

- The commonest way of showing a relationship between words is to use *of*:

e.g.   a cup of tea; the end of the road; the first day of the month

- The basic meaning of *off* is 'away from'. It is also the opposite of *on*.

e.g.   Keep off the grass. = Do not tread on the grass.

- We associate *off* with movement:

e.g.   They set off early.

b   *in | into; out | out of*

- We use *into* (= one word) when we want to show where someone or something has gone:

56

e.g. He slipped and fell in.
He slipped and fell into the pond.

● We use *out of* when we want to show from where someone or something has come:

e.g. He got out.
He got out of the taxi.

B

Task 1 Complete each gap with *of* or *off*.

1 She took a packet .... biscuits .... the shelf.
2 He took .... his shoes and put on a pair ....
slippers.
3 They've cut .... our electricity!
4 She broke .... a piece .... chocolate and gave it
to me.
5 She didn't believe a word .... his story.
6 The teacher rubbed the words .... the board.
7 He ran .... with the ball.
8 The ball rolled .... the table.
9 He bought a roll .... film.
10 We got .... the bus because it was full ....
noisy football supporters.   Score: /14

Task 2 Complete each gap with *in* or *into*.

1 He walked .... and sat down.
2 He walked .... the room and sat down.
3 He got .... and drove off.
4 He got .... the car and drove off.
5 She went .... the kitchen and made a sandwich.
6 She dived .... the swimming pool.   Score: /6

Task 3 Complete each gap with *out* or *out of*.

1 She threw him ....
2 She threw him .... the house.
3 He rushed .... the room and ran after her.
4 He rushed .... and followed her down the corridor.
5 The bird flew .... the window and disappeared.
6 He jumped .... bed.   Score: /6

26 Silent letters

•••

A

As we have seen in previous units, the sound of a word in English does not necessarily indicate how that word will be spelt. This is particularly true of words with silent letters (= letters that are not pronounced). To aid your spelling, it is very important that you should be aware of the most common words with silent letters.

> **Task**

Look carefully at the sets of words below. Pronounce each set of words and decide which letter in each word is silent. Write that letter in the space provided. The first set has been done as an example. Once you have completed this task, you will have created your own reference section for this unit.

Note: In the final set of words, there are two silent letters.

Silent letter

1   i̲sland; i̲sle   ..s̲..

2   listen; castle; soften; fasten; kitchen; watch;
    match; fetch; catch; switch; butcher   ....

3   answer; wrap; sword; wrist; wreck; wrong; write   ....

4   government; environment; autumn; column; hymn   ....

5   debt; doubt; plumber; climber; dumb; lamb;
    thumb; crumb; comb   ....

6   which; where; whether; honest; ghost; character; whisper   ....

7   know; knit; knee; knock; knot; knife   ....

8   guard; guarantee; guess; guide; guitar   ....

9   scientist; scene; scent; muscle; scissors   ....

10 handkerchief; Wednesday; sandwich; judge; hedge; adjust ....

11 cupboard; receipt; psychology   ....

12 could; would; should; half; salmon   ....

13 bought; caught; ought; thought; daughter; light;
    night; neighbour; straight; through   ....
                                                                                            (two letters)

Now check your answers and then go straight on to **B**.

B

Spot the mistake

How many spelling mistakes can you find in the sentences below?
Underline and correct every mistake you find.

1   The ship was recked in the storm.

2   We climed to the top of the hill were there was an old casle.

3   I wanted to wach television, but my mum told me to go strait to bed.

4   I wasn't sure wether she woud like it, so I bout her something else instead.

5   My teacher was not happy when I gave her the rong anser.

6   She said that the goverment was not doing enough to protect our enviroment.

7   We couldn't find a pair of sissors, so we had to use a nife.

8   I went into the kichen and made myself a cheese sanwich.

9   There's a tin of samon in the cuboard.

10 "Wich caracter in the book do you like best?" the teacher asked.

11 The children lisened to the gost story with open mouths and beating hearts.

12 He tied a not in his hankerchief to remind himself that his next gitar lesson would not be until the following Wensday.   Score: /28

Task 2   Spelling test

Ask a friend to test you on some of the words listed on the previous page.
Your friend should pick ten words and say them aloud. Your task is to
write them down correctly.

A

| Task 1 |

Complete the sentences below with *to*, *too* or *two*.

1   The shoes were .... big for him.
2   We went .... Birmingham .... see our cousins.
3   I have .... brothers.
4   "Are you coming .... my party?"
    "Yes. Can my brother come .... ?"
5   You're speaking .... quickly!

| Task 2 |

Complete the sentences below with *there*, *their* or *they're*.

1   .... ready.
2   Who's sitting .... ?
3   ....'s a fly in my soup!
4   They forgot .... books.
5   Have you met my brothers? .... standing over ....

| Task 3 |

Choose the correct alternative in brackets.

1   I didn't (hear / here) anything.
2   She's got a (saw / sore) throat.
3   We are not (allowed / aloud) to fish in this lake.
4   She has (fair / fare) hair and (blue / blew) eyes.
5   (Which / Witch) one do you prefer?

Now check your answers and then consult the **Reference** section before going on to **B**.

Reference

a   In written English, it is very easy to confuse one word with another if they sound the same.

e.g.   pair/pear; hair/hare; knew/new; hear/here

If you are ever in doubt, check the spelling of a word in a dictionary.

b Be particularly careful with *to* / *too* / *two* and *there* / *their* / *they're*.

- We use *to* in front of a <u>verb</u> (to go), a <u>noun</u> (to bed) or a <u>pronoun</u> (to him). On the other hand, we use *too* in front of an <u>adjective</u> (too small) or an <u>adverb</u> (too quickly). We can also use *too* to mean 'as well'. Finally, we use *two* when referring to the number 2.

- We use *there* either to introduce a noun (there's a fire) or to call attention to where something or someone is (over there). On the other hand, we use *their* to show 'possession' (it's their car) and *they're* as the shortened form of *they are*.

B

Task 1

There is one spelling mistake in each of the sentences below. Find and correct each mistake.

1 We're going to meat them later on this evening.
2 We went down to the beech and stayed there all morning.
3 I dropped the vase, but fortunately it didn't brake.
4 The train went threw the tunnel.
5 We had stake and chips for lunch.
6 It was to hot to go out, so we stayed in the hotel.
7 They said they wood wait for us.
8 We mist the bus and had to get a taxi.
9 For this recipe, you will need some flower and two eggs.
10 I had two peaces of cake and a glass of lemonade.   Score: /10

Task 2

Choose the correct alternative in brackets.

1 The (hole / whole) class went to the seaside.
2 I told him not to (stare / stair) at me.
3 Can you (sew / sow) on this button for me, please?
4 I love (leak / leek) soup.
5 The dog wagged its (tale / tail).
6 She says she (nose / knows) the truth.
7 It was a (waist / waste) of time.
8 Is this boat for (sail / sale)?
9 She said that she felt too (week / weak) to continue.   Score: /9

28 Some confusing words

A

Task

Select the correct alternative in brackets.

1 I was (quite / quiet) surprised to see them there.
2 We haven't decided (weather / whether) to go or not.
3 Make sure that you don't (loose / lose) this book.
4 Why did you (chose / choose) that carpet?
5 You need to (practise / practice) more.
6 Everybody is here (accept / except) Usman.
7 I'm not sure where they are. They (may be / maybe) upstairs.
8 I am older (than / then) Akram.
9 We had strawberry ice-cream for (desert / dessert).
10 She walked straight (past / passed) us without saying a word.

Now check your answers and then consult the **Reference** section before going on to **B**.

Reference

Certain pairs of words are particularly confusing. Some words look alike and therefore are easily confused or, as we saw in the last unit, they sound alike but are spelt differently. Look carefully at the examples and explanations below. Pay particular attention to (e).

(a) She's a very quiet child. (= 'not noisy')
    He played quite well. (= 'rather', 'fairly')
(b) What awful weather! (referring to the sun/rain/wind etc.)
    I don't know whether to go or not. (= 'if I should go or not')
(c) I think that we are going to lose the match. (= 'not win')
    The screw is a bit loose. (= 'not tight', 'not fixed properly')
(d) I don't know which one to choose. (= 'pick', 'select')
    He chose the green one. (the past tense of 'choose')
(e) I have to practise for another half an hour. (a verb)
    You need more practice. (a noun)*

   * With certain words you should remember that *s* means that the word is a verb (e.g. to advise, to practise, to license, to devise) and *c* means that the word is a noun (e.g. a piece of advice; hours of practice; a driving licence; a device for measuring things).

(f) He wouldn't <u>accept</u> any money. (= 'agree to take')

It is open every day <u>except</u> Sunday. (= 'apart from')

(g) <u>Maybe</u> he is ill. (= 'perhaps')

He <u>may be</u> ill. (= 'might be')

(h) We had some soup first and <u>then</u> a hamburger. (= 'after that')

She is younger <u>than</u> me. (*than* shows that a comparison is being made)

(i) They got lost in the <u>desert</u>. (= 'an area of land with very little rain')

What's for <u>dessert</u>? (= 'sweet', 'pudding')

(j) We <u>passed</u> the shop. (= 'went past')

We went <u>past</u> the shop. (= 'by')

B

Task 1

Choose the correct alternative in brackets.

1   I have to (practise / practice) the piano every day.
2   It takes a lot of (practise / practice) to play the piano well.
3   Could you give me some (advise / advice) on the matter?
4   Could you (advise / advice) me on the matter?
5   I found his (advise / advice) very useful.
6   Do you have a television (license / licence)?
7   He has invented a (devise / device) for catching flies.
8   We will have to (devise / device) a plan.   Score: /8

Task 2

Look carefully at each word that has been underlined. If it is correct, tick it. If it is wrong, correct it.

1   She was as <u>quiet</u> as a mouse.
2   I am <u>quiet</u> sure that she took it.
3   He was so <u>quite</u> that we didn't notice him.
4   I doubt <u>weather</u> he will come this evening.
5   I don't know <u>whether</u> he wants to come or not.
6   Some of the tiles on the roof are a bit <u>loose</u>.
7   It doesn't matter <u>weather</u> you win or <u>loose</u>.
8   We have to <u>chose</u> a new captain for our team.
9   Everybody was invited <u>accept</u> Paul.
10   She's not in the house. She <u>maybe</u> in the garden.
11   <u>May be</u> she's in the garden. Shall we have a look?
12   Peter says he <u>maybe</u> late this evening.
13   He's a better footballer <u>then</u> me.
14   The restaurant was very expensive, so we didn't have any <u>dessert</u>.
15   Go <u>passed</u> the church and <u>than</u> turn right.   Score: /17

29   Look, lock, lack, lake …

A

Task 1

In each sentence there is one incomplete word. Complete the word with *-ke* or *-ck* so that the sentence makes sense.

1   We weren't very hungry, so we just had a sna........ .
2   She screamed when she saw the sna........ .
3   Don't li....... your plate!
4   I didn't li....... the film.
5   I've hurt my ba........ .
6   We're going to ba....... some potatoes.

Task 2

Look carefully at the two groups of incomplete words. In one group the words should end in *-k*. In the other group the words should end in *-ck*. Which group is which? Can you work out a spelling rule with regard to *-k* and *-ck*?

Group A	Group B
lo.......	loo.......
so.......	soa.......
blo.......	boo.......
sho.......	shoo.......
che.......	chee.......

Now check your answers and then consult the **Reference** section before going on to **B**.

Reference

a   At the end of a word you may find either *-ke* or *-ck*. The sound of the word should help you to choose the correct ending.

e.g.   *-ke*: snake, bake, like, lake, sake, rake, bike, broke
-ck: snack, back, lick, lack, sack, rack, brick, black

b   At the end of a word, you may find *-k* or *-ck*.

• The letter *-k* follows <u>two</u> vowels:

e.g.   look, shook, break, book, week, weak, cheek, meek, leak, creak

• The letter *-k* follows a vowel + <u>consonant</u>:

e.g.   thank, trunk, sink, ask, task, risk

- The letters *-ck* follow a <u>single</u> vowel:

e.g.   lock, sock, track, trick, check, crack, neck, stuck, knock

Note: The letters *-ck* are also found in the middle of a word. The same rule applies: *-ck* is found after a single vowel.

e.g.   stocking, chicken, pocket, racket, rocket, bucket, jacket

c   Once you know the spelling of a short word, remember that the *-k* or *-ck* will not change when you make it into a longer word.

e.g.   li<u>k</u>e - li<u>k</u>ed - li<u>k</u>ing; li<u>ck</u> - li<u>ck</u>ed - li<u>ck</u>ing; kno<u>ck</u> - kno<u>ck</u>ed - kno<u>ck</u>ing; ris<u>k</u> - ris<u>k</u>y; lu<u>ck</u> - lu<u>ck</u>y; brea<u>k</u> - brea<u>k</u>fast; pa<u>ck</u> - pa<u>ck</u>ed - pa<u>ck</u>age - pa<u>ck</u>et

B

Task

There is one spelling mistake in each of the sentences below. Underline and correct each mistake.

1   He put on his tracsuit and went for a run.
2   She told him to change his dirty soks.
3   She locked out of the window.
4   You are jocking, aren't you?
5   He was as thin as a rack.
6   He was as proud as a peacook.
7   He kicked the ball too hard and brocke a window.
8   After breckfast, we went for a walk.
9   The child was knoked down by a lorry.
10   We bought two cakes and a paket of biscuits.
11   We paked our suitcases.
12   On Christmas Day I looked in my stoking and got a really nice surprise.
13   We had chiken for lunch.
14   A group of boys attacked us.
15   We thancked her for her kindness.
16   It was very cold, so I put on a jaket.
17   He craked his whip and the lion jumped through the hoop.
18   I looked through all my pockets, but I couldn't find the tiket.
19   He showed us a few triks.
20   I was really shoked when she told us what had happened.   Score: /20

Is it 'freind' or 'friend'?

A

Read the jokes below and select the correct alternative in brackets.

1 My (niece / neice), (Shiela / Sheila), has a very sweet tooth. One day she entered a restaurant and ordered a whole chocolate cake for lunch.

"Shall I cut it into four (pieces / peices) or eight?" asked the waitress.
"Four," she said. "I am on a (diet / deit)."

2 (Neil / Niel): Doctor, please help me. I can't stop telling lies.
Doctor: I don't (beleive / believe) you!

3 The bats were hanging upside down from the (cieling / ceiling) of a cave. All except one, who was hanging with his head upwards.

"That's a bit (wierd / weird), isn't it?" whispered one bat to another. "What's the matter with your (friend / freind)?"
"Be (quiet / queit)!" whispered the other bat. "He's taken up yoga."

Now check your answers and then consult the **Reference** section before going on to **B**.

Reference

a The rule '*i* before *e* except after *c*' is useful, but not always true. We need to be very careful when following this particular rule.

● We should first learn that normally *i* goes before *e* when the sound is *ee*.

e.g. believe, brief, chief, field, fierce, grief, niece, piece, priest, relieve, shield

● Let us now extend the rule. We should learn that *i* goes before *e* except after *c* when the sound is *ee*.

e.g. ceiling, deceive, receive, receipt

● Having learnt this rule, let us now look at the main exceptions (all written with *ei*). Learn these exceptions by heart:

protein, seize, weird, Keith, Sheila, Neil

b The second rule that we should learn is that we write *ei* when the sound is a long *a*.

e.g. neighbour, rein, reign, vein, veil, weigh, eight

c A third useful rule is that we write *ie* after *c* or *t* when the sound is *sh*.

e.g. ancient, species, efficient, sufficient, patient

d When *i* and *e* are separate sounds, the spelling is straightforward.

e.g. diet, drier, science

e Finally, some words we simply have to learn by heart.

e.g. friend, foreign, leisure, neither

B

Task 1   Complete each word with *ie* or *ei*.

1 th.......f; 2 v.......l; 3 n.......ghbour; 4 anc.......nt; 5 f.......ld;
6 rec.......pt; 7 n.......ther; 8 for.......gn; 9 w.......ght;
10 effic.......nt   Score: /10

Task 2   Read the following jokes and select the correct alternative in brackets.

1 Teacher: Name one animal that lives in Lapland.
(Kieth / Keith): A (reindeer / riendeer).
Teacher: Good. Can anyone name another?
Bill: Another (reindeer / riendeer)!

2 Tim: Doctor! Doctor! I think I'm getting smaller!
Doctor: Well, you'll just have to learn to be a
         little (patient / pateint).

3 After weeks of (fierce / feirce) fighting and long marches, the
(soldiers / soldeirs) were dirty, hot and tired. One day, the
(Chief / Chief) of Staff – General Armstrong – announced:

"My men, I have some good news and some bad news for you.
The good news is that you will each be (recieving / receiving)
a complete change of clothing."
"Hurrah!" chorused the men.
"And now for the bad news. Smith, you will change with Jones.
Jones, you will change with Brown. Brown, you will change
with Baker. Baker ... ."   Score: /7

Answer key

Unit 1

A

Task 1 The fastest land mammal in the world is the cheetah. It can reach speeds of over sixty miles per hour.

Task 2 Lions are sociable creatures. They live in families rather than in big herds as other animals do. In each family group there are between six and twenty animals.

Task 3 Snakes are cold-blooded creatures. They are only as hot or cold as the air around them. That is why you don't find many snakes in cool countries such as Britain. It's simply too chilly for them to stay alive.

B

Task 1
1 What is her name?
2 What a surprise!
3 How embarrassing!
4 How did it happen?
5 Do you know the answer?
6 Do it now!

Task 2

Come and enjoy a relaxing holiday at the Dolphin Hotel. It is very near a clean beach and there are plenty of shops nearby. The hotel is situated in a quiet area and has its own large swimming pool.

The rooms are spacious and clean, and each one has its own private bath and shower with hot and cold water. There is a colour TV in each room and a telephone if you want to call room service.

Our staff are friendly and we offer a high level of service. You will find everybody helpful and cheerful. There is always someone at the reception desk to help you with any problems.

The hotel has two lifts. There is a lounge with comfortable armchairs and a wide selection of newspapers and magazines. The hotel bar never closes before two in the morning.

(Score: 11 capital letters and 11 full stops)

Unit 2

A

Task
1 "Have you seen Suzy recently?"
   "No, I haven't seen her for ages."
2 "I am sure I know you," he said.
   "I think you are mistaken," she replied.
   "Aren't you Tariq's sister?" he asked.
   "Yes, I am," she said.
3 "That jacket looks nice," she said. "Can I try it on?"
4 "Please do not touch that vase," he said. "It's extremely valuable."

B

Task 1 He looked at her and said, "Where did you get that from?"
"I found it," she said. "It was on the floor."
"I don't believe you!" he shouted at the top of his voice.
"There's no need to shout," she said in a firm voice.
"Give it to me," he growled, "or you'll be sorry!"

(Score: 2 marks per line; for each mistake, lose ½ mark)

Task 2 Two small boys were discussing their future.

"What are you going to be when you grow up?" one of them asked.
"A soldier," answered the other.
"What if you get killed?"
"Who would want to kill me?"
"The enemy."
The other boy thought this over.
"Okay," he said. "When I grow up, I'll be the enemy."

(Score: 2 marks per sentence; for each mistake, lose ½ mark)

Unit 3

A

Task The following words should start with a capital letter: Thomas Smythe, Sheffield, April, Bono, French, Spanish, Spain, English, 'Slick Girls', Sheffield United, England.

B

Task 1 a Tuesday, Wednesday, Thursday, Saturday
b February, April, July, August, October, December

Task 2 1 She is Japanese.
2 He is Spanish.
3 He is Scottish.
4 He is Australian.
5 She is Nigerian.

Task 3 1 My brother, Tony, is a doctor. He lives in Wales and he speaks Welsh fluently. We usually see him at Christmas and, sometimes, at Easter.
2 For many years it was thought that the Nile was the longest river in the world. In 1969, however, it was finally decided that the mighty Amazon in South America was 4,195 miles long, fifty more than the Nile.

(Score: 15 capital letters and 5 full stops)

Unit 4

A

Task 1 1 "Yes, but I can't go."
"The invitation says 4 to 7, and I am eight."
2 "Waiter, there's a dead fly in my soup."
"Oh dear, it's the hot water that kills them."
3 "Dad, will you do my homework for me?"
"No, it wouldn't be right."
"Well, at least you can try."

Task 2 1 For breakfast I had orange juice, bread, jam, six sugar lumps, hot chocolate and two crispy things.
2 The train stopped in Milan, so we had to drive to Toscalano. We got there at siesta time and everything was shut, so we had to wait a while.

B

Task 1 "What's bright purple, has twenty-four legs, and ears that stick two inches out of its head?"
"I don't know either, but there's one crawling up your arm."

Task 2 1 The moon has no atmosphere and no water, so no life is possible.
2 People have been mining gold, silver, tin, iron, copper and lead for thousands of years.

69

3 Scientists have discovered that bees, mosquitoes, wasps and other stinging insects prefer to sting girls rather than boys.

4 It started to rain, so we stopped playing tennis.

5 He was wearing a pink shirt, green trousers and white shoes!

Unit 5

A

Task 1 A comma cannot be used to join two sentences. We should keep the two sentences separate or we should use 'joining' words.

1 I was sweating. I felt really uncomfortable. / I was sweating and I felt really uncomfortable.

2 I hate Keith. He is such a nasty boy. / I hate Keith because he is such a nasty boy.

Task 2 We can use a comma in 1, 3 and 5: When she heard the news, she burst into tears. / If it stops raining, we'll go for a walk this afternoon. / As he came nearer, I became frightened.

B

Task 1
1 I didn't like the film. It was boring. / I didn't like the film because it was boring.

2 I don't like Karen. She's so bossy. / I don't like Karen because she's so bossy.

3 You should eat fruit. It's good for you. / You should eat fruit because it's good for you.

Task 2
1 When I get to Paris, I'll give you a ring.

2 no comma

3 If you don't do your homework, your teacher will be annoyed.

4 no comma

5 no comma

6 As soon as I have enough money, I am going to buy a bike.

7 As it was getting late, we decided to turn back.

8 no comma

9 no comma

10 While we were waiting for a bus, we saw two foxes.

11 Just as I was leaving, the postman arrived.

12 no comma

Unit 6

A

Task 1
1 beds - brothers - sisters - pens - places - shoes

2 coaches - brushes - buses - dresses - boxes

3 ladies - babies - bodies - copies - hobbies

4 keys - donkeys - boys - toys - holidays

5 loaves - halves - calves - knives - thieves

Task 2 We should not use an apostrophe to make a noun plural. The plural of chip is chips. The plural of friend is friends.

B

Task
1 wolves
2 elves, goblins, fairies
3 stories
4 witches
5 cities, villages
6 Octopuses
7 wives
8 butterflies, countries
9 gases
10 galaxies
11 leaves
12 sandwiches, bunches, bananas, sausages, biscuits
13 puppies

Unit 7

A

Task 1 In each set of nouns, the odd one out is the one that ends in -*es*.
a photos - <u>heroes</u> - videos
b <u>tomatoes</u> - kilos - kangaroos
c pianos - <u>potatoes</u> - studios
d rhinos - hippos - <u>echoes</u>

Task 2 mice - geese - oxen - feet - teeth - women - children

Task 3 The underlined words are plural. They are strange because they can be used as singular nouns as well.

B

Task 1
1 Zoos
2 Kangaroos
3 mice
4 hippos
5 Tomatoes
6 potatoes
7 heroes
8 Rhinos
9 tornadoes/tornados

10 mosquitoes/mosquitos
11 volcanoes/volcanos
12 kilos
13 photos

Task 2 a herd of oxen; a gang of workmen; a gaggle of geese; a flock of sheep; a set of false teeth

Unit 8

A

Task 1 Four apostrophes are needed: We're having; The weather's been; it's beginning; you're enjoying.

Task 2 "I dont know." = "I don't know."

B

Task 1 Three apostrophes are needed: I'm glad; I wasn't; I can't.

Task 2
1 doesn't
2 They're
3 That's
4 There's
5 it's
6 Who's
7 I've
8 She's
9 weren't
10 shouldn't
11 Let's ... everything's
12 didn't ... hadn't

Unit 9

A

Task 1 a 2, 3 b 1, 4

Task 2
1 The <u>boy's</u> clothes = the clothes <u>of one</u> particular boy.

2 The <u>boys'</u> clothes = the clothes <u>of more than one</u> boy.

Task 3 1 at the doctor's = at the doctor's surgery.

2 doctors = more than one doctor.

B

Task 1 my uncle's house
2 Kevin's jacket
3 Shelley's room ... Anna's
4 the optician's
5 My parents' holiday
6 Fatima's party
7 lady's hat
8 Mrs Smith's face
9 Derek's eyes
10 Fiona's sister ... Surinder's glasses
11 the thieves' hiding-place
12 my grandfather's armchair

(Score: one mark per sentence)

Unit 10

A

Task 1 1 yours
2 ours
3 Hers
4 theirs

Task 2 1 Who's
2 Whose
3 There's
4 theirs
5 its, its

B

Task 1 1 his
2 hers
3 ours
4 yours

Task 2 a 1 Who's
2 Whose
3 Whose
4 Who's
5 whose
b 1 its
2 It's
3 It's
4 its, its
c 1 There's
2 theirs
3 theirs
4 There's

Unit 11

A

Task 1 The verbs in the passage are: have, catches, drops, escapes, grows, are, bury, is, keep.
All the verbs are in the present tense. If a verb ends in -s, this tells us that one person or thing (he/she/it) is performing the action or being described by the verb.

Task 2 1 plays
2 cries
3 pays
4 worries
5 enjoys
6 stretches
7 watches

B

Task 1 have, breathe, goes, are, passes, carries, pass, breathe
2 makes, lays, chooses, look, takes, leaves, flies, returns, has, is, hatch, creates, forces, feeds, cares
3 goes, carries, starts, does, eats, rises, uses

Unit 12

A

Task 1. a writing b moving c using
2. a running b swimming
   c stepping
3. a raining b feeling c peeling
4. a tidying b studying c crying

B

Task 1. pouring
2. copying
3. worrying
4. hopping
5. digging
6. cheering, clapping
7. slipping, sliding
8. arguing
9. having
10. hiding, hitting
11. planning
12. setting
13. shining, freezing
14. joking
15. trying, getting

Unit 13

A

Task 1 We know that the verbs are in the past tense because they all end in *-ed*.

Task 2 1. clapped, cheered, roared, started
2. skidded, crashed
3. studied, tried, failed
4. died, reigned
5. stared, nodded, smiled
6. stayed, played
7. said, paid

B

Task 1. enjoyed
2. said, fancied
3. begged
4. cheated, copied
5. slapped
6. cried
7. stepped, dropped
8. buried
9. laid, prepared
10. robbed, escaped
11. prayed
12. disobeyed
13. married
14. fired, missed
15. contained
16. annoyed
17. tapped
18. banned
19. poured
20. rubbed

Unit 14

A

Task 1 1. bought
2. brought
3. crept
4. heard
5. felt

Task 2 The verbs in 1 and 3 are in the present tense. The verbs in 2 and 4 are in the past tense. These particular verbs do not have a separate past form.

B

Task 1 1. caught, found, got
2. stung, hurt
3. thought, lost, fought, won
4. spread, burst

5 held, slid
6 kept
7 bent, split
8 taught
9 stuck, made
10 spent, built, could

Task 2 1 bilt = built
2 thougt = thought
3 struk = struck

Unit 15

A

Task 1 fell
2 fallen
3 bit
4 bitten
5 began
6 begun
7 hid
8 hidden
9 drank
10 drunk

B

Task 1 1 sang
2 sung
3 spoken
4 run
5 forgot
6 forgotten
7 saw
8 swam
9 sank
10 did
11 done
12 ridden
13 taken
14 came, took
15 stole

Task 2 1 tore
2 knew
3 written
4 flew
5 blew
6 chose
7 wore
8 shook
9 broke
10 beaten

Unit 16

A

Task 1 An adjective is a word that describes something or someone.
1 silly, these, lovely
2 This, terrible, sorry
3 pretty, intelligent, little

Task 2 1 tuff = tough; greasey = greasy; awfull = awful
2 funney = funny
3 beautifull = beautiful

B

Task 1 hungry
2 angry, horrible
3 awful, wonderful
4 wavy, rosy
5 straight
6 cheerful, nasty
7 noisy
8 stony, rough
9 difficult, runny, terrible
10 tasty
11 possible
12 painful, necessary

Unit 17

A

Task

1. boring
2. interested ·
3. amazing
4. satisfied
5. amusing
6. amused
7. annoyed
8. annoying
9. pleasing
10. pleased
11. worrying
12. worried

B

Task

1. surprised
2. excited
3. boring
4. terrifying
5. no mistake
6. embarrassing
7. embarrassed
8. no mistake
9. shocked
10. disgusting
11. satisfied
12. horrified
13. frightening
14. disappointed
15. no mistake
16. worried

Unit 18

A

Task

1. impossible
2. illegal
3. irregular
4. dishonest

5. unusual
6. unimportant
7. unnecessary
8. immature
9. impatient
10. invisible

B

Task

1. inefficient, ungrateful, inconvenient, incurable, informal, uneven, inexpensive, unfair, inaccurate
2. impolite, unpopular, unpleasant, impatient
3. irresponsible, unreliable, unreasonable, illegible, illiterate, unlucky
4. disobedient, unsatisfactory, disrespectful, disloyal, unfortunate

Unit 19

A

Task 1

1. warmer
2. larger
3. fatter, fitter, stronger

Task 2

1. smallest, largest
2. prettiest
3. laziest

B

Task

1. smaller, lighter
2. biggest, taller
3. saltier
4. thinner, harder
5. busiest
6. hottest, driest, coldest, windiest
7. widest
8. cheapest, easiest

9 dirtiest
10 smaller, shorter

Unit 20

A

Task 1
1 beautifully
2 carefully
3 quietly, calmly
4 heavily

Task 2
1 slow = slowly
2 real = really
3 easy = easily
4 gentle = gently

B

Task
1 immediately
2 angrily
3 accidentally
4 incredibly
5 Luckily
6 fantastically
7 completely
8 probably
9 desperately
10 terribly
11 possibly
12 usually
13 Suddenly
14 happily
15 Unfortunately
16 normally

Unit 21

A

Task 1
1 strength
2 length
3 weight
4 height

Task 2
1 visitor
2 gardener
3 conductor
4 butcher
5 burglar
6 spectator
7 lawyer
8 actor
9 teacher
10 liar

B

Task 1
1 traitor
2 beggar
3 prisoner
4 doctor
5 inspector
6 player
7 operator
8 traveller
9 sailor
10 pensioner
11 instructor
12 robber
13 swimmer
14 decorator
15 skier

Task 2
1 length, strength
2 height, weight
3 depth
4 width

Unit 22

A

Task 1
1 which
2 who
3 who
4 which
5 who

Task 2	1	who
	2	whose
	3	whose
	4	who

Task 3	1	who
	2	Who
	3	whom
	4	Who
	5	whom

B

Task	1	which
	2	who
	3	which
	4	which
	5	who
	6	whose
	7	Who
	8	whom
	9	which
	10	who

Unit 23

A

Task	1	The thing that annoys me … / What annoys me …
	2	I didn't see anybody. / I saw nobody.
	3	She doesn't know. / She does not know.
	4	A dishwasher is a machine that washes dishes.
	5	Susan, Ayesha, Sarah, Kiran and I went …
	6	I don't remember anything. / I remember nothing.
	7	My brother and I go swimming every Saturday.
	8	We were robbed!

B

Task 1	1	that
	2	What
	3	that
	4	What
	5	that
	6	that

Task 2	1	nobody
	2	anybody
	3	nothing
	4	anything
	5	no
	6	any
	7	I
	8	me
	9	were
	10	doesn't

Unit 24

A

Task 1	1	"I don't know who did it." / "I do not know who did it."
	2	"I want to be a pop star."
	3	"Who's going to tell her?" / "Who is going to tell her?"
	4	"I've got to go now." / "I have (got) to go now."
	5	"Are you all right?"

Task 2	1	fursday = Thursday; toofache = toothache
	2	fought = thought; bruvver = brother
	3	firty = thirty

Task 3	The words should be spelt as follows:
	1 a village
	2 the cinema
	3 a present
	4 a description

5   to decide
6   a suitcase
7   ten minutes
8   an English dictionary
9   English grammar
10   the town centre

B

Task	
1	all right
2	already
3	message
4	luggage
5	definitely
6	opposite
7	camera
8	favourite
9	television
10	grammar
11	theatre
12	thin
13	with
14	separate
15	responsible

Unit 25

A

Task 1	
1	of
2	off
3	of
4	off
5	off

Task 2	
1	He threw it <u>out of</u> the window.
2	He took a shirt <u>out of</u> the drawer.
3	They pushed him <u>into</u> the pond.
4	He jumped <u>into</u> the river.

B

Task 1	
1	of, off
2	off, of

3   off
4   off, of
5   of
6   off
7   off
8   off
9   of
10   off, of

Task 2	
1	in
2	into
3	in
4	into
5	into
6	into

Task 3	
1	out
2	out of
3	out of
4	out
5	out of
6	out of

Unit 26

A

Task	
1	s
2	t
3	w
4	n
5	b
6	h
7	k
8	u
9	c
10	d
11	p
12	l
13	gh

B

Task 1
1 wrecked
2 climbed, where, castle
3 watch, straight
4 whether, would, bought
5 wrong, answer
6 government, environment
7 couldn't, scissors, knife
8 kitchen, sandwich
9 salmon, cupboard
10 Which, character
11 listened, ghost
12 knot, handkerchief, guitar, Wednesday

6 *first* to = too
7 wood = would
8 mist = missed
9 flower = flour
10 peaces = pieces

Task 2
1 whole
2 stare
3 sew
4 leek
5 tail
6 knows
7 waste
8 sale
9 weak

Unit 27

A

Task 1
1 too
2 to, to
3 two
4 to, too
5 too

Task 2
1 They're
2 there
3 There
4 their
5 They're, there

Task 3
1 hear
2 sore
3 allowed
4 fair, blue
5 Which

B

Task 1
1 meat = meet
2 beech = beach
3 brake = break
4 threw = through
5 stake = steak

Unit 28

A

Task
1 quite
2 whether
3 lose
4 choose
5 practise
6 except
7 may be
8 than
9 dessert
10 past

B

Task 1
1 practise
2 practice
3 advice
4 advise
5 advice
6 licence
7 device
8 devise

Task 2
1 correct
2 quite
3 quiet

4 whether
5 correct
6 correct
7 whether, lose
8 choose
9 except
10 may be
11 Maybe
12 may be
13 than
14 correct
15 past, then

Unit 29

A

Task 1
1 snack
2 snake
3 lick
4 like
5 back
6 bake

Task 2 The words in Group A should end in -ck (lock, sock, block, shock, check). The words in Group B should end in -k (look, soak, book, shook, cheek). The letters -ck follow a single vowel. The letter -k follows two vowels.

B

Task
1 tracksuit
2 socks
3 looked
4 joking
5 rake
6 peacock
7 broke
8 breakfast
9 knocked
10 packet

11 packed
12 stocking
13 chicken
14 attacked
15 thanked
16 jacket
17 cracked
18 ticket
19 tricks
20 shocked

Unit 30

A

Task
1 niece, Sheila, pieces, diet
2 Neil, believe
3 ceiling, weird, friend, quiet

B

Task 1
1 thief
2 veil
3 neighbour
4 ancient
5 field
6 receipt
7 neither
8 foreign
9 weight
10 efficient

Task 2
1 Keith, reindeer, reindeer
2 patient
3 fierce, soldiers, Chief, receiving